Rev. Kartik Pal has done a scholarly study on "Disability and Sin in Christianity and Hinduism." He has studied the subject exegetically, theologically, and historically. It is not often that theologians look at such a topic and this makes Kartik's contribution unique. His work shows evidence of careful research and thought-provoking responses. The comparison of disability and sin in Christianity, specifically in the Old Testament, and Hinduism, makes the study even more relevant to the present context. His study helps readers to understand why these two major religions have different responses to this phenomenon. It is also a reminder that the religious presuppositions that people embrace outwork themselves through one's life, responses and actions. In India, there is a changing attitude to persons who are differently abled. Hopefully, Rev. Pal's study will inspire more dialogue on this important subject and that the church will be blessed to have a fresh understanding of disability.

– Rev. Dr. Matthew Ebenezer
Former Principal, Presbyterian Theological Seminary
Dehradun

Kartik Pal has given us a thorough work in looking at the difficult topic of Disabilities. His detailed historical research, as well as his thoughtful approach at viewing the topic from various perspectives, leaves the reader with much to ponder. This book provides a much-needed manuscript for society in general and workers in the field in particular.

– Linda L. Hutchinson
Church Planting International

"Kartik Pal compellingly contrasts attitudes of Christianity and Hinduism to disability and sin. It is a refreshing challenge to compassion in a context soaked with the idea of 'getting what you deserve.'"

– Dr. Ian W Payne
PhD, Executive Director, Theologians Without Borders
Former Principal, SAIACS, Bangalore

This book by Kartik Pal has taught me a great deal! Though I was raised in a Christian home and grounded in the Bible from childhood, I had never previously been exposed to the relevance of the Old Testament books of Leviticus and Deuteronomy in regard to understanding current topics such as the issue of disabilities. In addition, Pal's in-depth study of other Biblical passages and his thoughtful analysis of Hindu teaching provide much-needed guidance for Indian Christians, and, indeed, for all followers of Christ, in the 21st century. It is too easy for all of us to pay attention to the loud voices of the society around us. This book reminds us that the Word of God needs to be the foundation for our attitudes and actions in every sphere of life.

– Virginia Strom

As a primer for "This-abled Theology," Kartik's study lays the foundation for education, mission, and Pastoral care for these three crore "less-privileged" Indians.

– Rev. Dr. Nimai Charan Suna
Principal, Life Theological Seminary
Bhubaneswar

Biblical Hermeneutics Rediscovered - 40

DISABILITIES AND SIN IN CHRISTIANITY AND HINDUISM

As Conceptualized in Old Testament

Kartik Pal

Christian World Imprints

First Published in 2021 by

Christian World Imprints
Christian Publishing & Books from India
C-3, Wazirpur Industrial Area
Delhi-110052
cwidelhi2017@gmail.com
www.ChristianWorldImprints.com
Phone: +91 11 41526079

ISBN: 978-93-5148-517-9 (HB)
ISBN: 978-93-5148-518-6 (PB)

Printed in India.

CONTENTS

Dedicated
to the Glory of God,
and to all who stand for the cause of disabilities

ACKNOWLEDGEMENTS

Thanks to SAIACS for giving me the privilege and scholarship to pursue my M.Th. study in the Old Testament. I also take immense pleasure to express my sincere thanks to all those who have encouraged me take up Master of Theology course at SAIACS and stood with me during the journey of this research writing.

It is my deep desire to thank Dr. Havilah Dharamraj, my mentor, for her constructive instruction and innovative guidance. She has been available constantly in guiding me and giving me necessary and prompt feedback as and when I needed it.

I would also like to express my thanks to Dr. Stephen Guest (Head of department, Old Testament) for his constant encouragement and timely reminders and Dr. Ian Payne (Principal of SAIACS) for his concerns and providing me needed resources. I am also grateful to all my teachers for their significant inputs throughout my studies. I also highly wish to thank all my fellow sojourners for their regular prayers and practical advice from time to time.

I am greatly indebted to Rev. Dr. Nimai Charan Suna (Principal of Life Theological Seminary, Bhubaneswar, Odisha) and the entire LTS family for their prayers, support and encouragement.

Special thanks to Linda Hutchinson, Dr. James Gaillard Romaine and Virginia Strom for editing my work. Huge amount of thanks to Rev. L. Pine, Pastor Ryan Roberts, Judith Payne, Cokie Courchene Westfall, Ruth Hewlett, Dennis and Barbara Thorp, Timothy Myland and Philip Anthony Rodriquez for empathizing with our situation and standing with us in our trials by their prayers, support and encouragement especially towards my youngest son Joshua who is with disabilities.

I want express my heartfelt thanks to my wife Ahalya, my two sons Caleb and Joshua for patiently sharing with me the pressures and struggles throughout the years of my study. We as a family have experienced God's special presence and His providential sovereignty in our journey at SAIACS. Therefore, all the glory and honour to Him and to Him alone.

ABSTRACT

Recognizing the dismal attitudes of Indian Christians towards disabled people, an attempt has been made in this book to study the perception of disabilities in its relation to both the Old Testament and present day Indian culture influenced by Hinduism. To challenge such attitudes, this book has focused on the significant engagement of the Biblical perspective of disabilities with the Hindu perspective, especially, as concerns the connection with disability as retribution for sin. After considering praiseworthy bodies and disabled bodies of the Old Testament, it was discovered that sin is not the real reason behind disabilities. Thereafter, taking a step towards a historical interpretation of Christianity, it was found that the belief that sin is behind disabilities has not been the predominant perspective of the ancient, medieval, modern, or post-modern church.

However, it is clear that sin is the strong reason behind disabilities when considering the law of *karma* in Hinduism. According to the principle of *karma*, a person is disabled because of his/her sin which was committed in a previous birth. So, disabilities are seen as a form of retribution. Then how retribution in Deuteronomy in the Old Testament is different from retribution in Hinduism was shown by a comparative study. It is clear that God's love, compassion, and His personal relationship with His people were predominant factors regarding retribution in the Old Testament.

Further, going through popular culture, it is found that not only Indian Hindus but Indian Christians associate sin with disabilities in their preaching and teaching. It is revealed that Indian Christians appear to be widely influenced by the *karmic* association of cause and effect. This influence undermines the Biblical point of view and does not seem to have been helpful for Indian Christian communities. Therefore, this research suggests that the application of the teaching of the Old Testament concerning disabilities would help to develop biblical attitudes towards disabled people.

PREFACE

Jesus answered, "It was not that this man sinned, or his parents, but that the works of God might be displayed in him." John 9:3 ESV

I first met Kartik Pal in 2016 and I soon discovered that he is a gifted Christian leader. He grew up in a Hindu family in a village in the very conservative Hindu district in Odisha, India. Odisha is an eastern Indian state on the Bay of Bengal and is known for its tribal cultures and its many ancient Hindu temples. The capital of Odisha, where Kartik lives today with his wife Ahalya, and two sons Caleb and Joshua, is Bhubaneswar, home to hundreds of temples.

Coming from a Hindu cultural background, having been marvellously converted, graduating from Presbyterian Theological Seminary (M.Div.), from SAIACS (M.Th.) teaching the Bible and Theology, founding and directing the Reformed Gospel Fellowship of pastors and evangelists, and being father to a son with severe disabilities, Kartik is uniquely qualified to write on this subject.

Kartik writes, "this book primarily aims to study, how the Biblical perspective of disabilities engages with the Hindu perspective especially in the area of sin." This is an important and difficult subject but one that Kartik addresses admiralty and I applaud him for taking it on.

I hope that more Christians both in India and elsewhere will study the subject of disabilities. There is so much more we need to learn. Our God is a gracious God who cares for and honors those who are weak. May each of us learn to be as gracious and compassionate in our treatment of and attitude towards the disabled as our loving Father, our Lord Jesus Christ and our Comforter, the Holy Spirit are.

It is therefore a great honor for me to write a preface for this book. May God bless you, encourage you, and inspire you as you read it.

Dr. James G. Romaine
Church Planting International

ABBREVIATIONS

AB	Anchor Bible
ACA	Apostolic Christian Assembly
AD	Anno Domini
ca	Circa, meaning around
CNN	Cable News Network
Deut.	Deuteronomy
DGS	Duraisamy Geoffery Samuel
DRC	Divine retreat Centre
EDAN	Ecumenical Disability Advocates Network
Ezek.	Ezekiel
Gen.	Genesis
IAS	Indian Administrative Service
IPC	Indian Pentecostal Church
Isa.	Isaiah
JCID	Journal of Christian Institute of Disability
JCNM	Jesus Christ of Nazareth Ministries
Jer.	Jeremiah
JETS	Journal of Evangelical Theological Society
Job	Job

Judg.	Judges
Lev.	Leviticus
NRSV	New Revised Standard Version
Num.	Numbers
OT	Old Testament
PMO	Prime Minister's Office
Prov.	Proverbs
Ps.	Psalm
Sam.	Samuel
WCC	World Council of Churches

Chapter 1

INTRODUCTION

1.1. The Issues

There is a growing interest in research among Indian Christians in the study of disabilities for three significant reasons. First, the Bible records the disabilities of man and as people of Scripture we cannot ignore them. In the Bible, there are various kinds of disabled persons which includes physical, intellectual, congenital. We also find many issues related to disabilities which cannot be underestimated. Second, God is concerned for persons with disabilities. The evidences of God's grace, love and compassion for the disabled in the Bible demands our close attention. Third, more significantly, we must know how to deal with disabilities in present day India.

It is significant to note that the emphasis on contextualization has been increasing in present day India. In the twenty-first century, we hear voices from Dalit theology, women's theology, tribal theology and many more. But, voices from disabled people are silent. As Wati Longchar reminds us "all these voices have been raised by the able-bodied people for the able-bodied persons."[1] But voices from the people with disabilities are "silent" in Christian "theological" reflection and "are raising new theological questions" now.[2] This indicates that people are now aware of this great need in the theological discourse and ministry of the church. Many are addressing this issue and writing to challenge Christians to approach the Bible and construct a theology from the perspective of persons with disabilities.

Moreover, in the present Indian Hindu society, disabilities are seen as the result of sin. A person is born with disabilities because of the sin he/she committed in a previous birth. People with disabilities are often considered inferior and worthless compared to other able-bodied persons. They are marginalized and discriminated against in Indian societies. As a result, they grow up with fear, anxiety and low self-esteem. People with disabilities are largely ignored by the Hindu society. Surprisingly, such treatment of disabilities not only comes from the Hindu community but even Christians in India have also developed the same attitudes as Hindus. Hence, this opens an opportunity to investigate the reason behind such attitudes and offer a biblical perspective which will provide a guide to the ways Indian Christians can respond to such a special need.

1.2. Purpose

This book primarily aims to study, how the Biblical perspective of disabilities engages with the Hindu perspective especially in the area of sin.

1.3. Introduction to the Chapters

In this book, there are five chapters. We will consider the Old Testament perspectives of disabilities and sin (Chapter 2), the

1 Wati Longchar, "Culture, Sin, Suffering and Disability in Society", *In Doing Theology from Disability Perspective: A Theological Resource Book on Disability 2011*, ed. Wati Longchar and Gordon Cowans (Philippines: The Association for Theological Institution in South East Asia, 2011), 175.

2 Longchar, "Culture, Sin, Suffering and Disability in Society", 175.

Historical Perspectives of Disabilities in Christianity (Chapter 3), the Hindu Concept of Sin and Disabilities (Chapter 4), and Disabilities, as viewed in Popular Hinduism and Indian Christianity (Chapter 5), aiming to gain a Biblical perception of disabilities and provide at the end a Biblical perspective for the Indian Christians.

In the first part of Chapter 2, while studying the Old Testament perspective of sin and disabilities we will consider both the praiseworthy bodies and disabled bodies. While studying the praiseworthy bodies we will try to discover whether sin is in anyway associated with disabilities. Descriptions of praiseworthy bodies are found in multiple places in the Old Testament. We will study the case of Rachel, Saul, and Samson. In considering the praiseworthy bodies, we will observe the function of physical attributes of the admirable protagonists in the narratives.

First, we will study the case of Rachel. Rachel's beauty is described in Genesis 29:17. But Robert L. Hubbard states that though she had abundant beauty yet she suffered the "shame of barrenness."[3] Secondly, we will study Saul's beauty as described in 1 Samuel 9:2. According to Michael Avioz Saul's physical features are appropriate "qualities" for a good leader but gradually he lost all the qualities.[4] Thirdly, Samson's exceptional ability to kill a lion is described in Judges 14:8-9. Amanda Beckenstein Mbuvi asserts that "Samson strikes a powerful blow in defense of Israelite covenantal integrity. However, he, himself is so caught up in Philistine Culture that gesture destroys him as well."[5]

We will conduct a detailed investigation of each of the above protagonists to find out the function of the bodily abilities and strength in the characterization mentioned in the narratives. The Old Testament concept of disabled physical bodies has been

---

3 Robert L. Hubbard, "The Eyes Have It: Theological Reflections on Human Beauty" *Ex auditu* 13 (1997): 59.

4 Michael Avioz, "The Motif of beauty in the books of Samuel and kings" *Vetus Testamentum* 59 (2009): 346.

5 Amanda Beckenstein, "Samson's Body Politic" *Biblical Interpretation* 20 (2012):405.

recorded in multiple places. While considering the disabled bodies we will take some of the major and relevant texts appropriate to our study.

In the second part of chapter 2, First, we will study Leviticus 21:17-23. A simple reading will give us an impression that disability is something God himself disapproves of, since there is a strong prohibition on the priests from making offerings in holy places if he has a disability. Daniel C. Koblitz agrees with C. Astor that the focus here was "primarily concerned with Israel being a pure representation of God than with a negative view of a priest's disability."[6] We need to explore if this view holds under careful exegesis.

Secondly, in Exodus 4:10-12 Moses complained about his inability to speak when God called him to carry out His task. Nyasha Junior and Jeremy Schipper assert that "modern interpreters" support this as Moses making an excuse to "escape" a task given to him by God and avoid having "a confrontation with Pharaoh."[7] But they also put forward, as a fact, that it is not an excuse, but actually Moses expressing his "disability", and God making a point from that He is sovereign over man's physical condition.[8] Along the same lines John Swinton asserts that "Within God's providence disability has deep meaning."[9] We will need to study the narrative closely to see what functions Moses' disability serves in the context of his calling to become Israel's deliverer.

Thirdly, in 2 Samuel 9:1-13 David invited the disabled descendent of Saul, Mephibosheth to eat at the king's table. It will be interesting to see what prompted David to do this. One

---

6 Daniel C. Koblitz "Theology and Disability: Reexamining Scripture as It Applies to Stuttering" *The Journal of the Christian Institute on Disability* (JCID) 5, no. 1 (Spring/Summer 2016): 36.

7 Nyasha Junior and Jeremy Schipper, "Mosaic Disability and Identity in Exodus 4:10; 6:12,30" *Biblical Interpretation* 16 (2008): 429.

8 Junior and Schipper, "Mosaic Disability and Identity in Exodus 4:10; 6:12, 30", 431.

9 John Swinton, "Many Bodies, Many Worlds" In Disability: Christian Reflection 2012, ed. Robert B. Kruschwitz (Waco: The Center for Christian Ethics Baylor University, 2012), 19.

point of view is that David's motivation was political. According to Christopher D. Rouse, David watches the grandson of Saul carefully by giving him a special position so that the plan of restoration of the "throne" will be "impossible."[10] Another point of view is that David is keeping his covenant promise to a Saulide. If this is the case Rod Thomson's view may be relevant. Thomson highlights the dimension of Deuteronomic covenant where he makes a point that the disability of Mephibosheth is due to "God's rejection and affliction of Saul and his family" and it should be seen in the context of "Deuteronomic covenant cursing."[11] He further makes a point that "David's embrace of covenantal kindness has overcome covenantal cursing, offering hospitality to one who would otherwise have been excluded, one who could have been dealt with as the enemy, the cursed, the unfit, the unwelcome."[12] We will need to engage this point of view with Thomas E. Reynolds and Frances Young who hold the opposite view that disability is not due to sin or fault. According to Reynolds and Young what matters is the relationship offered to people with the disability.[13] By the end of this chapter we will have considered narratives of both abled and disabled persons and reached a conclusion on whether the OT makes an association between the physical body and sin. With this done, we will next investigate if there is a historical association between sin and disabilities made by the church.

The objectives in this chapter is to investigate the historical perspectives between disabilities and sin in Christianity. This

---

10 Christopher D. Rouse, "Scripture and the Disabled: Redeeming Mephibosheth's Identity" *Journal of Pentecostal Theology* 17 (2008): 190.

11 Rod Thomson, "Mephi Bosheth at the table: A High Point in Davidic Kingship-2 Samuel 9:1-13" *In Theology and the Experience of Disability, 2016*, ed. Andrew Picard and Myk Habets, New York: Routledge Taylor & Francis Group, 2016, 150.

12 Thomson, "Mephi Bosheth at the Table: A High Point in Davidic Kingship-2 Samuel 9:1-13" 151.

13 Thomas E. Reynolds, "The Cult of Normalcy" In Disability: Christian Reflection 2012, ed. Robert B. Kruschwitz (Waco: The Center for Christian Ethics Baylor University, 2012), 26.

endeavor will cover three different periods: Ancient Church History from AD 30-AD 590, Medieval Church History from AD 590-AD 1517 and Modern Church History from AD 1517-till today.

In the period from AD 30- AD 590 the early Church may or may not have been influenced by Jewish thinking. Patricia Bruce states that "in Jewish society" there was a strong association "between disability and sin."[14] Moreover, Elaine Ledgerwood and Carol Thomas agree that in "Judeo-Christian" culture disabilities were considered as "divine punishment."[15] However, A. Brooke Blanks and J. David Smith observed that the early church unlike the Hebrew understanding looked at disability as not divine punishment but as a medium through which God's "mercy and power" are revealed.[16] We will study to find out whether the belief that sin is behind disabilities was a predominant factor in ancient Christianity.

In the period from AD 590-AD 1517, according to Carole M. Cusack, "the medieval Christian culture" thought disabilities were a divine punishment for sinfulness, but that was "not the only interpretation which was wide spread."[17] This indicates that medieval Christianity had multiple perspectives with regard to disabilities. Ledgerwood states that though the connection between disability and sin formed a foundation and became a disgrace for the people with "disabilities" yet the written records of the "saints" (biographies of saints who have experienced disabilities) raises a question about such a concept in the medieval

14 Patricia Bruce, "Constructions of Disability Ancient and Modern: The Impact of Religious Belief on the Experience of Disability" *Neotestamentica* 44, no. 2 (2010): 277.

15 Elaine Ledgerwood, "Saint not Sinners: An Investigation into the "Positive" Constructions of Disability by the Historical Church" *Colloquim* 42, no.1 (May 2010): 92.

16 A Brooke Blanks and J. David Smith, "Multiculturalism, Religion and Disability: Implications for special Education Practitioners" *Educational and training in Developmental Disabilities* 44, no. 3 (2009): 298.

17 Carole M. Cusack, "Graciosi: Medieval Christian Attitudes to Disability" *Disability and Rehabilitation* 19, no. 10 (1997): 418.

church.[18] It seems like the belief that sin is behind disabilities had already formed a stigma in the medieval Christianity. But, we will investigate whether sin is the sole reason accepted as the cause of disabilities throughout the Medieval Christianity.

In the period of the Reformation from AD 1517 onwards we will consider the perspectives of reformers like Martin Luther and John Calvin towards disabilities. In the post-reformation period on the one hand, scholars like David Andrus,[19] A Brooke Blanks and J. David Smith,[20] David Deuel,[21] and Daniel Daniel C. Koblitz[22] had a negative response towards disabilities. On the other hand, another set of scholars such as Andrus,[23] Andrus,[24]

---

18 Ledgerwood, "Saint not Sinners: An Investigation into the "Positive" Constructions of Disability by the Historical Church", 85.

19 David Andrus observes that after the reformation of 16th century "the new way of thinking amplified the belief that physical disabilities are the result of sin. (David Andrus, "Theology and its Impact on People with Disability: An Ecclesiology Inclusive of People with a Disability" *Missio Apostolica* 18, no. 2 (Nov. 2010): 143.

20 Blanks and Smith asserts that Martin Luther considered children with disability are not "human" but they are "incarnation of devil." (A Brooke Blanks and J. David Smith, "Multiculturalism, Religion and Disability: Implications for special Education Practitioners" *Educational and training in Developmental Disabilities* 44, no. 3 (2009): 298.

21 David Deuel asserts that due to sin "pain, suffering, disability and even death" came to this world. (David Deuel, "God's Story of Disability: The Unfolding Plan from Genesis to Revelation," *The Journal of Christian Institute of Disability* (JCID) 2, no. 2 (Fall/Winter 2013): 82.

22 Koblitz asserts that Bible relates original sin released sin into the world including disease, disability and death. (Koblitz "Theology and Disability: Reexamining Scripture as It Applies to Stuttering", 35.

23 Andrus gives his opinion that the disability due to the fall is not necessarily correct since the whole creation is affected due the fall into sin. (Andrus, "Theology and its Impact on People with Disability: An Ecclesiology Inclusive of People with a Disability"143.

24 Andrus further explains that such an understanding holds a "false idea that some people are more sinful than the others." (Andrus, "Theology and its Impact on People with Disability: An Ecclesiology Inclusive of People with a Disability" 143.

David[25] had a positive response towards disability. It appears then, that, there is diversity of opinions throughout church history when it comes to the connection of disabilities with sin. We will investigate therefore the connection of disability with sin in each period of Church History. By the end of this chapter we will have considered the association of disability and sin in Ancient, Medieval and Modern Church History.

Having done this, we will look at the Hindu concept of sin and disabilities in the fourth chapter. We will explore whether there is a connection between disabilities and sin in Hinduism. In order to understand this comprehensively we will give close attention to the study of sin and karma in Hinduism in connection with disabilities.

As concerns the connection between sin and disabilities, scholars don't have any unity of thought. On the one hand, some give their opinion that there is no connection between sin and disabilities. Sarah Whitman gives a sense that disability is not a punishment for sin.[26] In fact, Ed. Viswanathan,[27] Paul Younger and Susanna Oommen Younger assert that there is no "doctrine of sin" in Hindu thought.[28] On the other hand, Bonela Ganpathi asserts that "disability is held to be punishment for the sins of a previous birth."[29] However, we can take the argument forward by considering whether there is a concept of sin in Hinduism. Thereafter, we will examine if sin is linked with disabilities.

---

25 Deuel further states that God takes the responsibility of the disable. Deuel, "God's Story of Disability: The Unfolding Plan from Genesis to Revelation" 85.

26 Sarah M. Whitman, "Pain and Suffering as Viewed by the Hindu Religion" *The Journal of pain* 8, no. 8 (August 2007): 609.

27 Ed. Viswanathan states that apart from mythology there is no concept of sin in Hinduism. (Ed. Viswanathan, *Am I a Hindu?* (New Delhi: Rupa & Co, 1993), 287.

28 Paul Younger and Susanna Younger Assert that there is no doctrine of sin the the Hindu system of thought. (Paul Younger and Susanna Oommen Younger, *Hinduism* (Niles Illinois: Argus communications, 1978), 36.

29 Bonela Ganapathi, "Rehabilitation for the disabled person," *International journal of Multidiciplinary Research Trends* III, no. 3 (July 2016): 52.

There is a strong belief which links physical disabilities to *karma*. For example M. Miles states that disability is understood "in terms of retributive consequence."[30] Sarah M. Whitman,[31] A. Praveen Prakash, J. Esther Jerlin and P. Anitha[32] strongly argue that physical disability is a part of unfolding *karma*. We will investigate whether such an argument is dominant in Hinduism. With this done, we will make a comparison between the law of karma and retribution in Deuteronomy.

Next, to achieve our purpose we will look at popular Indian culture of both Hindus and Christians through popular media in the fifth chapter. We will consider popular literature, daily newspapers reports, Bollywood movies, You Tube videos and other related media to see how Indians in general seem to view disabilities and display their attitude. Here we will then try to make a link between the traditional philosophical Hindu position and the popular Indian attitude towards disabilities.

Popular culture also has a great influence on Indian Christians since the Indian Christian community has significant interactions with the rest of the Indian society on various issues of culture and community. So, it is likely that Indian Christians also view disabilities in the same way as Indian Hindus. We will look at the popular preaching and teaching of Indian Christians on You Tube videos and establish whether such a claim is true. Having examined that, at the end of this chapter, we will provide a Biblical corrective to such an attitude among Indian Christians.

---

30 M. Miles, "Disability in an Eastern Religious Context: Historical Perspectives," *Disability and Society 10*, no. 1 (1995): 61.

31 Whitman asserts that according to Hindu philosophy "physical" disability is "part of unfolding karma." Whitman, "Pain and Suffering as Viewed by the Hindu Religion" 609.

32 According to A. Praveen Prakash, J. Esther Jerlin and P. Anitha "Physical disability is thought to be part of the unfolding karma." (A. Praveen Prakash, J. Esther Jerlin and P. Anitha "Dominent Problems of Rural Deprived Persons with Disability Using Fuzzy Cluster Analysis. Proceeding of the World Congress on Engineering 1 (July 2-4, 2014): np.

1.4. Methodology

Since I will deal with the narratives of the Hebrew text, I will employ the literary exegetical analysis of the relevant selected text from the Old Testament. In addition to this, we will examine several case studies from the Old Testament narratives. We will primarily use the tools of narrative criticism. Next, historical research will be adopted to study the historical interpretation and perspectives of churches towards disabilities. Finally, a comparative study of the concept of disabilities in both the Old Testament and Hinduism will be done, as the chief strategy, to accomplish the purpose of the thesis. This book will be an interdisciplinary study investigating certain Old Testament concepts in the light of Church History and moving to a parallel concept in Hinduism. Field research will not be taken into consideration to understand the popular Indian conceptions on disabilities.

Chapter 2

OLD TESTAMENT PERSPECTIVE OF DISABILITIES AND SIN

2.1. Introduction

Since the Old Testament is the foundation of the Christian scriptures, our central focus in this chapter is to discover the relationship between physical disabilities and sin in the Old Testament. Many scholars have puzzled over the Old Testament concept of disabilities. David Deuel asserts that due to sin "pain, suffering, disability and even death" came into this world.[33] Deuel further asserts that "disability is a high price of living in a sin-cursed world."[34] However Koblitz asserts that disability falls in

33 Deuel, "God's Story of Disability: The Unfolding Plan from Genesis to Revelation", 82.

34 Deuel, "God's Story of Disability: The unfolding Plan from Genesis to Revelation", 83.

the plan of God.[35] Does that mean God is the source of disability? Indeed, it is confusing.

People with disabilities face discrimination since the connection between sin and disabilities has formed a stigma in the minds and hearts of the people. This chapter will analyze the biblical perspectives of sin and disabilities. It will investigate whether there is a connection in the Old Testament between the human body and sin. That means we will seek to verify whether disabilities in the Old Testament is in any way related to sin. Relevant texts for an exegetical study which could answer this question come under two opposite categories: the praiseworthy bodies, and the disabled bodies.

2.2. Praiseworthy Bodies in the Old Testament

The human body is considered praiseworthy usually because of its beauty or extraordinary ability. We will pick Old Testament narratives in which protagonists are admirable for these reasons. Then we will study the narrative to see how the physical attributes function within the narrative.

2.2.1. The case of Rachel: Genesis 29-30

First, we will study the case of Rachel. The beauty and barrenness of Rachel is famous in the narrative accounts of Genesis. Rachel appears in the narrative when Jacob was sent by his parents to find a wife from among the women of his mother's family. Jacob went on a long journey and as he approached Haran he came upon a well which was in the field. It was at that well Jacob met Rachel, and it is worth noting what happened when Jacob met Rachel for the first time. Jacob kissed Rachel first and then he introduced himself, whereas usually the introduction takes place first. It seems Rachel was beautiful and Jacob loved Rachel at first sight.

Moreover, Rachel is described as being beautiful compared to Leah. The description of both the sisters focuses on their physical attributes. "Leah was tender eyed; but Rachel

35 Koblitz, "Theology and Disability: Reexamining Scripture as it Applies to Stuttering", 34.

was beautiful" (יְפַת־תֹאַרהָיְתָהוְרָחֵלרַכּוֹתלֵאָהוְעֵינֵי) (Gen. 29:17). L. Daniel Hawk asserts that "the meaning of the Hebrew phrase here translated "weak eyes" is obscure but it cannot be complementary."[36] Whereas E. A. Speiser states that tender eyes does not mean "weak" eyes but the point the narrative makes here is "Leah had lovely eyes, but Rachel was an outstanding beauty."[37] William A. Dyrness states that the Hebrew word here "yappa" (יָפַת) means to be "fair/beautiful" and usually describes a person's physical beauty which is visible from outside.[38] Besides that Hawk further asserts that Rachel had a "striking figure and striking appearance."[39] Robert L. Hubbard asserts that the description of both the sisters shows a clear contrast between "Leah's single appealing feature (her eyes)" and "Rachel's striking overall beauty."[40] The glowing description of Rachel by the narrator suggests that she was shining physically.

It is significant to note that the narrator is describing the physical attributes of both of the sisters before Jacob asks for Rachel in marriage. At this point, we are clear that Rachel's superior beauty caused Jacob to love her and prompted him to determine his subsequent actions for 7 years (Gen. 29:18), which seemed like just a few days to him (Gen. 29:20). But, Laban tricked Jacob into marrying Leah who was actually not loved by Jacob. Jacob was deceived by Laban on the wedding night and instead of getting married to Rachel he married Leah. But even after the marriage, Jacob loved Rachel more than Leah (Gen. 29:30). The narrator has emphasized Jacob's love towards Rachel

---

36 L. Daniel Hawk, "Cast Out and Cast off: Hagar, Leah and the God who sees" *Priscilla Papers* 25, no. 1 (Winter 2011): 11.

37 E. A. Speiser, *Genesis*, AB, (New York: Doubleday & Company, Inc, 1985), 225.

38 William A. Dyrness, "Aesthetics in the Old Testament: Beauty in Context" *Journal of the Evangelical Theological Society* 28, no. 4 (December 1985): 424.

39 Hawk, "Cast Out and Cast off: Hagar, Leah and the God who sees" 11.

40 Hubbard, "The Eyes Have It: Theological Reflections on human beauty", 58.

by repeating the phrase "Jacob loved Rachel" three times in the narrative (Gen. 29:18, 20, 30). Robert L. Hubbert states that Leah's "shortage of beauty" not the "beauty deficit" became the real reason behind her not being loved.[41] It suggests that the narrator has intentionally described the physical attributes of Rachel and Leah to show that not only was Rachel beautiful but also that men value women because of their beauty and physical attractiveness.

However, infertility troubles beautiful Rachel. The LORD's intervention throws a different light in the narrative. The fact is that the LORD does not see the way men see. He did not just look at the outward beauty of Rachel. The LORD by being gracious and mindful of the situation intervenes on behalf of Leah who was unloved. As per Gen. 29:31 the LORD opened Leah's womb because he saw she was hated. But Rachel was barren. It seems like God has closed the womb of Rachel.

The divine intervention of opening the womb is remarkable in the narratives of the Old Testament. Sarah said to Abraham "Yahweh has kept me from bearing" (Gen. 16:2) literally restraining. Similarly, in the case of Hannah "Yahweh had closed her womb" (1 Sam. 1:5). Notice Jacob's response to Rachel, "Can I take the place of God who has denied you fruit of the womb" (Gen. 30:2). Joel S. Baden states that the words "restraining", "closing" and "withholding" are used as "rhetorical devices" in the narratives to demonstrate the "opposition" between Sarah and Haggar, Hannah and Peninah, and Leah and Rachel.[42] In each case directly or indirectly Yahweh has opened the womb of one and closed the womb of other.

Baden further asserts reflecting on some Biblical texts (Ps. 105:41; Isa. 50:4-5; Ezek. 3:27; Num. 22:28) that the act of YAHWEH in opening "something" is a sign of "transformation"

---

41 Hubbard, "The Eyes Have It: Theological Reflections on human beauty" 59.

42 Joel S. Baden, "The Nature of Bareness in the Hebrew Bible" in Disability Studies and Biblical Literature 2011, ed. Candida R. Moss and Jeremy Schipper (United States: A division of St. Martin's press LLC, 2011), 16.

from ordinary to extraordinary.[43] Rachel's longing to be a remarkable woman, in spite of her physical beauty, is not possible since her womb is closed. Elana Bloomfield states that "within many traditional Jewish texts women's bodies are portrayed as fertile vessels."[44] In such circumstances Rachel's infertility evidently troubled her. John Dekker states that though there is no explicit expression of God closing Rachel's womb yet the implication clearly indicates that.[45] Hawk also strongly asserts, observing the degradation of Leah "the LORD opened her womb but closed the womb of Rachel."[46] It appears on the surface that the LORD is not kind to Rachel.

The significance of barrenness can be only clearly understood when we reflect upon the socio-cultural ideology of the Jewish people. Rachel's urgency in getting children can be drawn directly from such a context. Bloomfield asserts that a Jewish woman's ability to bear children plays an integral role in building the nation as well as its necessity to survive.[47] Producing children provides a mother significant value in the Jewish family, society, and nation. In fact, Bloomfield further states that a woman's fertility gives her a special recognition and place in the society.[48] And it gives us the idea that a woman without children has no identity in the Jewish society. Moreover, Charles Savona Ventura asserts that "fertility was particularly directed towards the agricultural and husbandry gifts of the so-called fertility deity that enable the survival of the

---

43 Baden, The Nature of Bareness in the Hebrew Bible, 15.

44 Elana Bloomfield, "Conceiving Motherhood: The Jewish Female Body in Israli Reproductive practices" *Intersections* 10, No. 2 (Spring 2009): 228.

45 John Dekker, "May the Lord Make the Woman like Rachel" *Tyndale Bulletin* 64, No. 1 (2013): 22.

46 Hawk, "Cast Out and Cast off: Hagar, Leah and the God who sees"11.

47 Bloomfield, "Conceiving Motherhood: The Jewish Female Body in Israli Reproductive practices" 229.

48 Bloomfield, "Conceiving Motherhood: The Jewish Female Body in Israli Reproductive practices" 232.

community."[49] This is part of a pagan idea. The demand for the high fertility is more due to better economy and better survival. This may be one of the reasons behind Rachel taking the image of a pagan household deity from her father's house. In addition to that Havrelock asserts that Rachel's inability to conceive points out a failure of the promise God gave to the patriarch.[50] God promised Abraham to give a land, a seed and a blessing (Gen. 12:1-3), echoed to Isaac (Gen. 23:3) and Jacob (Gen. 28:13). Obviously female infertility is then a great hindrance to such a promise.

It is in this above description context that bearing children for a Jewish mother seems more forceful. Obviously then women with children are more honored whereas barren women are degraded in the Jewish society. By bearing children a woman can contribute towards building the family, the nation, and the economy and Rachel at this point is absolutely helpless. She is troubled for not being able to contribute towards the family, nation and economy in spite of her praiseworthy physical structure. Having enjoyed the affection of her husband because of her physical attractiveness she now experiences degradation, humiliation, and childlessness.

Eventually after failing to conceive a child, Rachel painfully has a confrontation with Jacob her husband in connection with her barrenness. Her infertility produced a bitter experience in this context whereas her sister could give Jacob four children. Her frustration and desperation can be noticed when she comes to Jacob and says, "Give me children or else I die" (Gen. 30:1). It reveals an envious spirit in Rachel. She envied her sister since she could not give any children but her sister could. Jacob responds with harsh words by saying, "am I God's stead, who has withheld from thee the fruit of the womb?" (Gen. 30:2). The word "withhold" or "deny" signifies "a lack of positive action rather than as denoting negative action."[51] Baden further states that both

---

49 Charles Savona Ventura, "Reproductive Issue in the Torah" *Malta Medical Journal* 27, No. 2 (2015): 47.

50 Rachel Havrelock, "The Myth of Birthing the Hero: Heroic Barrenness in the Hebrew Bible" *Biblical Interpretation* 16, (2008): 155.

51 Baden, The Nature of Bareness in the Hebrew Bible, 16.

Leah's fertility and Rachel's infertility are determined by divine intervention.[52] Moreover, Rachel also brings her maid Bilhah as a surrogate mother because of the delay in her having a child. It is permissible as Kayla White states that one of the legal acts of a barren woman is to encourage her husband to take a second wife in order to secure her future.[53] Though, for Rachel taking this step is legal yet it involves quite a risk since her own status can be despised as Sarah was despised by her own handmaid Hagar (Gen. 16:4-6). Hagar was a humble maid servant of Sarah in spite of the fact that she was barren. But when she conceived, her whole perception towards Sarah was changed. Anna Goldman Amirav states, the more "dominant figure in the ancient near east religion" were those women who have the ability to bear children.[54] Rachel being without children can easily be despised by her maid.

The narrator makes clear that Rachel at this point was in deep anguish and heartache because of her infertility though she gave birth to two sons sometimes later. This means that in spite of her physical beauty Rachel suffered degradation, shame, rejection and grew jealous. Robert L. Hubbard states that though she had abundant beauty yet she suffered the "shame of barrenness."[55] The case study of Rachel is not explicit about the fact that her bareness is due to any specific sin but it definitely reveals her character flaws. She is envious of Leah's fertile womb and manipulative in introducing surrogacy as a means to motherhood. We may infer from this that the narrator's characterization of Rachel physical beauty does not indicate either the blessing or approval of God.

---

52 Baden, The Nature of Bareness in the Hebrew Bible, 14.

53 Kayla White, "The Legal Status of barren Women in the Ancient Near East" *Priscilla Papers* 28, No. 4 (Autumn 2014): 18.

54 Anna Goldman Amirav, "Behold the LORD has Restrained Me from Bearing" *Journal of International Feminist Analysis* 1, No. 3 (1988): np.

55 Hubbard, "The Eyes Have It: Theological Reflections on human beauty", 59.

2.2.2. The case of Saul: 1 Samuel. 9-31

Secondly, let's study the case of Saul. The Old Testament has given much space to describe this narrative as it begins in 1 Samuel 9, where Saul appears in searching for his father's donkey and ends in 1 Samuel 31, where he throws himself on his own sword after being wounded by the Philistines. The research in this section will focus on the function of Saul's praiseworthy body in the narrative. Saul's psychical structure, character and conduct will be taken into consideration. Saul's praiseworthy body is described in 1 Samue 1.9:2. He was a "good" (טוֹב) young man as compared to the people of Israel. He stood head and shoulders above everyone else (1 Sam. 10:23). Saul is described as choice, handsome and more personable than anyone in the land. Further on many occasions he has been represented as the one chosen by God (1 Sam. 10:24, 24:10, 2 Sam.1:14).

To see Saul's character, we must look at the way Saul responded to the divine offer. Saul did not want to become king but still he became a king. It proves that God is sovereign in his choice. But Saul's response to his divine election is clear from the way he expressed his inadequacy. When he confronted Samuel (1 Sam. 9:21), and his uncle (1 Sam. l0:14-16) he was afraid to speak of the kingship and when he was confronted by the nation he hid in the baggage (1 Sam. 10:20-22). This gives us a glimpse of Saul's internal character. It seems like his assumptions of a king were more influenced and inspired by the idea of Mesopotamian civilization of that ancient period. Frankfort asserts that in Mesopotamian civilization the king was a "Sumerian lugal means great-man."[56] Saul did not accept the divine offer to become king because he had a wrong assumption that human suitability and attributes are essential to be a king. He based his reluctance to become king on his family background. It gives us a sense that Saul gave more value to human criteria to become a king than God's sovereignty. This particular standing led Saul to disobey

56 Henry Frankfort, *Kingship and the Gods: A Study of Ancient Near Eastern Religion as the integration of Society and Nature* (Chicago: The University of Chicago Press,1978), 6.

God later. Bill Crowder states that Saul's reliance on "external appearance" without internal character is the invitation to his downfall.[57] Crowder further strongly asserts that in spite of the fact that Saul was a provision of God yet his spiritual character is questionable.[58]

To examine Saul's conduct, we will study the text to see the cause of the divine rejection of the king Saul. In 1 Sam.13:13 Samuel says Saul is foolish in not keeping the commandment of God and consequently his kingdom will not continue. In 1Samuel 15 Saul spares the life of the Amalekite king for which he is told that Yahweh is not pleased and his sense of rejection of Saul being king is very strong. In 1 Samuel 28:16-28 Saul seeks a medium to consult Samuel who is dead and the spirit of Samuel tells him that Yahweh has become his enemy due to how he dealt with Amalekites. All these texts center on the burning issue of Saul's disobedience to God's command to destroy the Amalekites which is the fundamental reason for God's rejection of Saul.

Yisca Zimran states that the matter of Saul's rejection comes out from Saul being pictured as the ideal king.[59] 1Samuel 15 records the command to Saul, by Samuel in God's name to attack the Amalekites and utterly destroy them and all that they have (1Sam.15:2-3). Zimran asserts that the verses are designed to give a picture of specific "injunction" and an "imperative" to obey.[60] In spite of the clear description of the decree and anticipation of the order Saul failed to obey the commandment of God. The Amalekites were killed but their king survived. The command was to destroy them all and that they had. But only what was cheap and worthless was destroyed. In doing so Saul violated all the particulars of the commands and put a question

57 Bill Crowder, *Poor Choices and Mixed Opportunities: The Mistakes of Saul* (Grand Rapids: RBC Ministries, 2010), 12.

58 Crowder, *Poor Choices and Mixed Opportunities: The Mistakes of Saul*, 12.

59 Yisca Zimran, "The Lord Has Rejected you as King Over Israel: Saul's Deposal from the Throne" *Journal of Hebrew Scripture* 14, no . 5 (2014): 2.

60 Zimran, "The Lord Has Rejected you as King over Israel: Saul's Deposal from the Throne" 5.

mark on his obedience. David M. Gunn states that Saul is accused of disobeying God, "pretending" to do what is "required" and blaming others for his own weakness.[61] Gunn also states that he is neither "humbled for his offence" nor prompted by the "goodness" of God to "repentance."[62] Gunn further asserts that Saul was controlled by his "will fulness", "selfishness", "passionateness" and "jealousy."[63] The effect of sin in Saul's conduct is very evident. Saul and the people were united in their effort to spare the Amalekite king and the other precious things instead of destroying them and obeying God. But Saul makes an excuse that it was the army who directed him not to destroy everything completely. He does not accept the blame but rather accuses others for something for which he is more responsible.

Moreover, Saul exceeded his authority in intervening in priestly matters by offering sacrifice. But Samuel refused to accept Saul's right to offer sacrifice. Arther E Cundall states that by this particular act is Saul is attempting to perform priestly "functions" just like "the kings of other nations."[64] Again Saul's endeavor to become a king like those of other nations has been highlighted, for which God is displeased.

Though it appears Saul's disobedient acts stand out as the chief reason behind Saul's deposal, yet observing the essential elements, the sin that caused Saul's rejection does not rest on either this or that but essentially in his character. He was not rejected just because of one sin. Other kings were forgiven when they sinned and repented. God is not responsible for His deterioration. His sinful character has been clearly demonstrated by the narrator. It is his sinful character that compels Saul to display sinful conduct. The narrator beautifully highlights his sinful character and conduct and shows that having a strong human body is not the sign of a pious man.

---

61 David M. Gunn, *The Fate of King Saul* (England: JOST Press, 1989), 42.

62 Gunn, *The Fate of King Saul*, 43.

63 Gunn, *The Fate of King Saul*, 43.

64 Arther E Cundall, "Sacral King-The Old Testament Background" *Vox Evangelica* 6 (1969): 35.

In considering his physical structure, there is a specific reason behind the people choosing Saul with such exceptional looks and ability. Crowder states that "since people wanted to be like other nations" God himself raised an able person without character like Saul.[65] God is quite intentional in order that the people would realize the failure of human ability. It indicates that physical structure without character is nothing. God just gave to the children of Israel what they wanted most.

Often people think the praiseworthy body of Saul is the criteria for God's choice. In fact, at a superficial level, though it appears that Saul was the choice of God yet when we go in the depth in the narrative we realize that Saul as a king was not the choice of God. David M. Howard states that it seems God allowed Saul to be king as a "concession" in response to the "sinful request" of the people.[66] God's displeasure concerning a human king is ambiguous in the Biblical texts. But it is clear that the function of Saul's praiseworthy body in this narrative does not occupy any special consideration in God's choice. It has been used by God only to meet the sinful request of the people. Avioz states that "tall king" Saul was used as a "puppet" in the hand of God and Samuel.[67] No doubt he had exceptional physical qualities but in the eyes of God it did not earn him any credit or condition. The real reason behind the disapproval of the request of the people was because they wanted a king just like all the other nations (1Sam. 8:5), who would judge, lead, and fight their battles (1Sam. 8:20). It is worth quoting Henry Frankfort who strongly asserts that in the ancient near east "security, peace, and justice" could only be achieved by a ruler.[68] It seems like people are convinced that it is

---

65 Crowder, "*Poor Choices and Mixed Opportunities: The Mistakes of king Saul*", 10.

66 David M. Howard, "The Case for Kingship in the Old Testament Narrative books and the Psalms" *Trinity Journal* 9, (1988): 19.

67 Michael Avioz, "The Motif of beauty in the books of Samuel and kings", 346.

68 Frankfort, *Kingship and the Gods: A Study of Ancient Near Eastern Religion as the Integration of Society and Nature* (Chicago: The University

the leader's abilities and physical strength which can make a real difference as they compare themselves to the surrounding nations. And Saul in terms of his looks brings a lot more excitement and hope to the minds and hearts of people. But Crowder makes a point that even though Saul is an appropriate candidate in terms of his appearance and "fit the mind and molds of the people" yet he is neither "God's first choice" nor fit for God's heart.[69] However, the people of Israel could see nothing more than Saul's outward appearance and celebrated it. The compelling argument is that physical attributes are not the basis of God's choice. It seems that visible outward appearance can be a matter of consideration for men but not for God. Despite the fact that Saul was the choice of people and not of God, yet God accomplished his purpose by making him the first king of Israel for no other reason than to show the people that they should look at the heart not the outward appearance of man (1Sam. 16:7).

2.2.3. The case of Samson: Judges 13-16

Thirdly, we will study the case of Samson. Samson is known for his long hair and extraordinary strength. He could defeat the entire armies of Philistines by himself. He could kill young lions and break thick rope. He was blessed with supernatural strength and handsome stature. His strength was from God. But he overlooked his need for God and lived as if he was the source of his own strength.

The narrative of Samson begins with highlighting the fact that Israel continued to do evil in the eyes of YHWH (Judg. 13:1). It is significant to note that the narrative of Samson in the Old Testament begins with a significant shift, "And "it happened" (וַיְהִי) (Judg.13:2). "It" indicates that something unusual is going to happen. Samson's mother was not clearly introduced but her state of bareness has been stressed by the narrator (Judg.13:2). In spite of her bareness she makes no effort like Sarah, Hannah and Rachel to have children. We do not know much about the

of Chicago Press, 1978), 3.

69 Crowder, *Poor Choices and Mixed Opportunities: The Mistakes of Saul*, 11.

situation and status of Samson's mother. To this Benjamin J. M. Johnson states that YHWH is the one who initiates Samson's narrative.[70] Samson was born in a miraculous way as per the announcement of an angel of the LORD (Judg.13:4). His life begins with great promise. The basic information about Samson is that he has to live a life of separation to God (Judg.13:5). Johnson asserts that the kind of life Samson had to live falls under the "Nazarite vow" described in Numbers 6:1-8.[71] Mark Green states that the central part of this "vow" is "separation" found "nine times in Numbers. 6:1-21."[72] This truly emphasizes the nature of separation. The narrator makes it clear that Samson's life is consecrated to the LORD even before his mother conceived. Three prohibitions are especially mentioned there: 1. abstaining from wine or strong drink, 2. having no razor touch the head and 3. having no contact with a corpse. This indicates that he is called to live a special life of service. The other information we get is the fact that he will deliver Israel from the power of Philistines (Judg. 13:5). At this point we get a clear picture of Samson's mission. Johnson asserts that though Samson's mission is clear from his "birth" yet he gives no attention to his unique "status before YHWH."[73] Samson's engagement to a Timnite woman is a real evidence of it. Robert Ball asserts that as per the Rabbinical law Samson should choose to marry only "from among the young maidens of Israel" and exclusively "Jewish women."[74] But he desired to marry a Philistine maiden from Timnah. Camille W. Slight asserts that intermarriage for Samson was not good since it

---

70 Benjamin J. M. Johnson, "What Type of Son is Samson? Reading Judges 13 as a Biblical Type-Scene" *JETS* 53, no. 2 (June 2010): 274.

71 Johnson, "What Type of Son is Samson? Reading Judges 13 as a Biblical Type-Scene" 277.

72 Mark Green, "Enigma Variations: Aspects of the Samson Story Judges 13-16," *Vox Evangelica* 21 (1992): 59.

73 Johnson, "What Type of Son is Samson? Reading Judges 13 as a Biblical Type-Scene" 278.

74 Robert Ball, "Christian Leadership and the Crippling Effect of Narcissism: A Historical Intertexture Analysis of Judges 13-16" *Journal of Biblical Perspectives in Leadership* 6, no. 1 (2014): 20.

would never help to "preserve true faith" and assemble the people of God.[75] Moreover, Samson asks his parents to arrange that marriage. James D Martin rightly states that the "usual" way to "arrange the marriage" ultimately falls in the hand of "parents."[76] But his parents objected since it was against the law (Deut. 7:1-3), and Philistines were uncircumcised (Judg.14:3a). Taking a wife from the uncircumcised Philistines is also a clear violation of his Nazirite status. Instead of listening to his parents' objection he commands them "Get for me" (קַח־לִי) (Judg.14:3b). Mark Green asserts that within the cultural context where children must obey their parents, this kind of behavior towards parents was absolutely dishonorable.[77] Samson is insensitive and disrespectful to his parents as well as God.

Judges 14:4 introduces a real shocking complication as the narrator explains Samson's act as having the approval of God. According to Judges 14:4 Samson's parents did not realize this was the LORD's doing. Of course, God works in mysterious ways which go beyond human understanding and often it contradicts the ways of man. But in this case, it gives the idea that what Samson is doing is right and his parents are not. It is significant that this verse should be understood in the overall purpose of God. In the context, the purpose of God is to bring down the Philistines for which he is still at work in spite of Samson's unfaithfulness. This verse does not offer a message that man always does right things but that God redeems us from our "misdeeds" and "sinful selves."[78] Samson's parents were perhaps much worried by the fact that by intermarriage with Philistine maiden from Timnah, he would spoil

75 Camille W. Slight, "A Hero of Conscience: Samson Agonistes and Casuistry" *Modern Language Association* 90, no. 3 (May 1975): 398.

76 James D. Martin, *The Book of Judges*, Cambridge Bible Commentary, (New York: Cambridge University Press, 1975), 161.

77 Green, "Enigma Variations: Aspects of the Samson Story Judges 13-16." 64.

78 J. Clinton McCann, *Judges: Interpretation: A Bible Commentary for Teaching and Preaching* (Louisville, Ky: Westminster John Knox Press, 2011), 102.

his Nazirite dignity without realizing that God still could redeem Samson's misdeeds and accomplish his purpose. However, it still questions Samson's unfaithfulness and misbehavior remains. In this respect, it gives a picture that God is gracious and faithful but Samson is rebellious and unfaithful. This verse states that God was seeking an occasion or opportunity (the NRSV says "pretext") against the Philistines (Judg. 14.4). But J. Clinton McCann asserts that God neither needs pretext nor waits for the opportunity or occasion to stand against the "oppression and injustice" of the Philistines because he "always opposes oppression"[79] So this verse cannot be understood as the approval of God on Samson's act, rather it demonstrates the questionable conduct of Samson.

Moreover, Samson did not explain when he killed a lion (Judges 14:6), and when he gave honey to his parents (Judges 14:9). His unwarranted presence in the vineyards violated the Nazirite vows. Being a Nazirite he should be away from "anything" that has to do with "wine and grapes (Num.6:1-4)."[80] But he did not give any serious attention towards it. He ate the honey and also gave some to his parents. The appearance of lion may be considered as warning from God to keep Samson "away" from breaking the vows.[81] But instead of getting the message from God he killed the lion. Having done all these things, he keeps them secret from his parents because he knows that "his parents" regard the "Nazirite status and God's purposes in general" more earnestly than "he himself does."[82] In this way he broke the Nazirite vows (Judges.14:16). Commenting on his attitude Michael J. Smith strongly states that Samson was "rebellious" to his parents.[83]

It is also crucial to note that while giving the reason for choosing his wife from Timnah Samson states that "she looks good to me" (בְעֵינַיְיָשְׁרָהכִּי־הִיא) (Judg. 14:3b). It seems the narrator

---

79 McCann, *Judges*, Interpretation, 102.

80 McCann, *Judges*, Interpretation, 103.

81 McCann, *Judges*, Interpretation, 103.

82 McCann, *Judges*, Interpretation, 103.

83 Michael J. Smith, "The Failure of the Family in Judges, Part 2: Samson" *Bibliotheca Sacra* 162 (October-December 2006): 430.

wants to show there is no difference between Samson and the "people of those days since the children of Israel did whatever was pleasing to their eyes" (יַעֲשֶׂהבְּעֵינָיוהַיָּשָׁראִישׁבְּיִשְׂרָאֵל) (Judg. 21:25). For Samson God's instruction and his parents' discernment have no value. In his eyes the Philistine maiden, she was a suitable and an appropriate wife for him. This demonstrates the clear tension between God's will and Samson's will. This kind of attitude encouraged Samson to develop a tendency to become careless in his entanglements with the Philistine women and eventually to fall in love with one more Philistine woman, Delilah. Robert Ball asserts that Samson's love affair with Delilah was sinful.[84] He had to pay for this open indulgence to sin. Taking advantage of this situation, the rulers of Philistines came to her and said that if she could tempt Samson into showing her the secret of his strength, they would give her eleven hundred shekels of silver. Responding to the request of Delilah, Samson revealed the secret and Philistine rulers easily bound him and put him in prison. He had such a tragic end since, though he was a leader, he did not see the clear direction of the Lord.

It indicates that although Samson had God-given supernatural strength, the effect of sin is clearly visible from his life. There was a progressive development to his open indulgence to sin. His continuous life of disobedience to God clearly indicates the effect of sin. Here again we see being divinely favored with physical ability does not have any correlations with his faithfulness towards God in leading an exemplary life in line with his calling.

2.3. The Disabled Bodies in the Old Testament

The Old Testament concept of the disabled physical body has been recorded in multiple places. Three major texts which are fundamental related to physical disability will be taken into consideration. These texts have made a significant impact in understanding disabilities in the Christian tradition and have

84 Robert Ball, "Christian Leadership and the Crippling Effect of Narcissism: A Historical Intertexture Analysis of Judges 13-16", 22.

created a legacy of negative perceptions at a superficial level. We will attempt to reproduce relevant implications after careful observation of these texts.

2.3.1. Leviticus 21:17-23

First, we will consider one of the crucial legal passages, Lev. 21:17-23, which addresses disabilities more directly and has been taken as a normative stand traditionally. In this text, we see the requirement of God to prohibit anyone with deformities from doing priestly activities at the altar. The Hebrew word (מֹום) means blemish (Lev. 21:17), or defect. From Lev. 17 to Lev. 21 we see who falls into the category of a man who has a defect. According to Michael S. Beates the word deformities includes "blind, lame, disfigured, deformed, crippled in hand or foot, hunchbacked, dwarfed, defective eyes, running sores."[85] At a superficial level it suggests that God is negative towards a priest with a disability and only a priest of perfect physical form can approach the altar and perform priestly work. Amos Yong taking one of the widespread hermeneutical approaches of evangelical standard asserts that this Levitical code must be dealt with "metaphorically" or "symbolically" instead of "literally" to get much deeper "universal principles" and "spiritual meaning."[86] Having stated this Yong makes a point that the text here does not encourage us to see disability as worthy of disgrace or disapproval from God but brings awareness of "spiritual deficiencies and waywardness" of people which defile the place filled with "divine holiness."[87] This view seems more appropriate when we understand the goal behind the exclusion. The whole purpose of the prohibition of a blemish priest is stated by the LORD himself that "he will not profane my sanctuary" (אֶת־מִקְדָּשַׁיְחַלֵּלוְֹלֹא), "because I am the LORD who sanctifies them" (מְקַדְּשָׁםיְהוָהאֲנִיכִּי) (Lev. 21:23). It

85 Michael S. Beates, *Disability and The Gospel: How God Uses Our Brokenness to Display His Grace* (Wheaton: Crossway, 2012), 30.

86 Amos Yong, *The Bible, Disability and The Church* (Grand Rapids: William B. Eerdmans Publishing Company, 2011), 25.

87 Yong, *The Bible, Disability and The Church*, 25.

indicates that this text is not negative towards disable people. It does not state disability is due to sin. But strongly focuses on the spiritual condition of people which is an obstacle in keeping their relationship with God. Considering the text within the Christological framework Yong stresses that "priestly prohibitions refer less to the Levitical bodies and function more as anticipating the Great High Priest who is Jesus" since the whole set of sacrificial laws of the Old Testament was fulfilled by Jesus as the Great High Priest.[88] Jesus is not only the perfect priest but also the perfect sacrifice. It questions who is the perfect priest other than Jesus. It is in Jesus that both the able and disabled find perfection. The focus of the text therefore is not on discrimination of disabled people but on essential characteristics of people while approaching to the holy place.

Beates further states that though the "disfigured" or "blemished priest" cannot perform priestly activities on the "altar" yet they can be priests and carry out some other responsibilities.[89] It was then only the service of the most holy places that were forbidden for them, where they had to enter the veil for priestly work (Lev. 21:23), not the eating of the sacrificial meal (Lev. 21:22). That means blemished priests were not completely barred from priestly activities. They could still enter the sanctuary where the portion for the priest was brought and shared and take part in the meal. How then could a priest with physical disability be considered impure and unworthy? If they were, then they should not take part in eating the portion from holy places. But they could still continue their priestly work, remain in the sanctuary and enjoy the provision of food from the holy offering. For Saul M. Olyan, this type of exclusion of the priest from the priestly work is only "partial."[90] Moreover, Olyan also states that a priest who has

88 Yong, *The Bible, Disability and The Church*, 26.

89 Beates, *Disability and The Gospel: How God Uses Our Brokenness to Display His Grace*, 30.

90 Saul M. Olyan, *Disability in the Hebrew Bible: Interpreting Mental and Physical Differences* (New York: Cambridge University Press, 2008), 31.

a "defect" is not socially discriminated against by the people.[91] As a priest he still got honour and respect in society.

Beates also asserts that instead of pulling out this text, it must be considered and "understood" in the whole context and within the "purpose" of Leviticus.[92] Then Beates finally makes clear that the goal of this passage is not to regard a disfigured person as "unworthy" but to show the "Holiness of God" to the people of Israel.[93] It is significant to observe the perspective of God towards disability within the book of Leviticus. The LORD said to Moses, "you shall not curse the deaf or put a stumbling block to the blind, but you shall fear your God, I am the LORD." (Lev. 19:14). Indeed, this unique perspective of God may be a big surprise to everyone. It is certainly not expected that the same God who will reject a disfigured person in the temple at the same time can show deep concern, respect and care for them. In addition to this Yong states that in the context of Leviticus 21-22 the primary focus is on laws to govern the priesthood.[94] In the context of these many laws, to target only disabilities would be injustice since the law of disabilities is only one among many such laws which excludes someone from performing priestly activities. It indicates that within the wider framework of the Leviticus, the condition of disabilities should not stand out. But the primary concern is that Israel should be the pure representation of God. So God is neither negative towards disabilities nor is sin the real cause behind them.

2.3.2. Exodus 4:10-12

Secondly, Moses and his disability will be taken into consideration. Though the text Exod. 4:10-12, is a very short text yet it is very profound and offers a significant perspective on disabilities

---

91 Olyan, *Disability in the Hebrew Bible: Interpreting Mental and Physical Differences,* 31.

92 Beates, *Disability and The Gospel: How God Uses Our Brokenness to Display His Grace*, 31.

93 Beates, *Disability and The Gospel: How God Uses Our Brokenness to Display His Grace*, 31.

94 Yong, *The Bible, Disability and The Church,* 19.

from the theology of the Torah. When God called Moses from the burning bush, Moses made several objections. The first three objections are found in Exod. 3:11, 13 and in 4:1. In the process of convincing God that he was not qualified to do God's work Moses made his fourth objection. Moses said "Oh my LORD, I am not a man of speech" (דְּבָרִיםאִישׁלֹאאָנֹכִי) (Exod. 4:10). Most English translation say "I am not eloquent." He gives a reason for it for "I am slow of speech and slow of tongue" (אָנֹכִילָשׁוֹןוּכְבַדכְבַד־פֶּהכִּי) (Exod. 4:10). Moses' description of his speech difficulty is also found in Exod. 6:12, 30 where he says he has "Uncircumcised lips" (שְׂפָתָיִםעֲרַל). So, he is heavy of speech with uncircumcised lips. Moses was reluctant to become God's spokesperson because his speech would be a great hindrance. His objection is obvious since he assumed that God would choose someone who would be fluent in speech to send to Pharaoh. Many and mostly modern scholars debate whether Moses had a disability in speech or was simply making an excuse. But Marc Sell states that some see it as "physical deformity linked with language disability."[95] In addition to that Nyasha Junior and and Jeremy Schipper in talking about Moses' reason for his "ineloquence" assert that he had a disability of speech.[96] They further state that the "focus" of "God's response" is also on his "disability."[97] Indeed, God's response is very direct and straight forward. God said to Moses, "who set the mouth for man"? (לָאָדָםפֶּהשָׂםמִי) or "who makes dumb or deaf, or seeing or blind"? (עִוֵּראוֹפִקֵּחַאוֹחֵרֵשׁאוֹאִלֵּםמִי־יָשׂוּם), "Is not I the LORD"? (יְהוָהאָנֹכִיהֲלֹא) (Exod. 4:11). We cannot miss the full impact of what God has said here. Beates asserts that God takes complete "responsibility" and "credit" for this disability.[98] It implies that God is sovereign in watching over the disabled.

95 Marc Sell, "Moses' Tongue", *Common Knowledge* 12, no.1, (2006): 153.

96 Junior and Schipper, Mosaic Disability and Identity in Exodus 4:10; 6:12; 6, 431.

97 Junior and Schipper, Mosaic Disability and Identity in Exodus 4:10; 6:12; 6, 431.

98 Beates, *Disability and The Gospel: How God Uses Our Brokenness to Display His Grace*, 29.

Deuel states that "Responsibility means that God is not just the cause, but the upholder, enabler, and final rescuer of people with disabilities."[99]

Another dimension of this text is to notice whether God uses Moses in his disability or heals him. It is surprising that God did not heal Moses so that he could do his task comfortably, but assured his own presence right at the point of Moses' disability as he sent him out to carry out his mission (Exod. 4:12). For Amos Yong, the LORD's response to Moses appears in the context as a real encouragement for Moses to stand "before Pharaoh" on behalf of the "people of Israel."[100] John Swinton asserts that "God uses disabled bodies to carry out key tasks of the coming kingdom"[101] It implies that the way God sees and uses disability is quite different than the way man sees things. Man may see the disabled as worthless and unfit and finally ignore them. But God lifts them up to a significant level and uses them in His mission. It is significant to note that in this text also an association between sin and disabilities is not found.

2.3.3. 2 Samuel 9:1-13

Thirdly, let us take Mephibosheth and his disability into consideration. He was the son of Jonathan and grandson of Saul who became crippled in both feet. His story is not found in one place but scattered throughout 2 Samuel (2 Sam. 16:4,19:24). But we will study 2 Sam. 9:1-13 where David in declares his desire to show kindness to Mephibosheth. David was at the height of his success when he showed mercy towards Mephibosheth. There was no war since he had defeated the Philistines, conquered Jerusalem and brought the ark to Jerusalem (2 Sam. 1-7:29). David now reigns and his kingdom is at peace. During such a time of success David said, "I will show mercy" (חֶסֶדעִמּוֹאֶעֱשֶׂה) (2 Sam. 9:1). It is indeed important to take note that normally people forget others during

99 Deuel, God's Story of Disability, 82.

100 Amos Yong, *Theology and Down Syndrome: Reimagining Disability in Late Modernity* (Texas: Baylor University Press, 2007), 22.

101 Swinton, "Many Bodies, Many Worlds" 19.

the height of their success but David brings Mephibosheth to his table, am man who considers himself like a dead dog (2 Sam. 9:8). Geoffrey David Miller asserts that though in ancient Israel a dog is viewed with contempt and some references in the Old Testament throws a "negative" picture towards dogs yet it is not consistent and prevalent throughout the scripture.[102] However, the sense we get it from this particular text is negative. For Deuel, David's act of not only providing "care" but giving privilege to Mephibosheth to sit at his table and treating him just like his "family member" was "more than a kindness."[103] For this attitude Rod Thompson strongly asserts that David must be "admirable."[104]

The motivation behind this admirable act is ambiguous. Scholars have many opinions. According to Christopher D. Rouse, David keeps the "grandson of Saul" to watch him carefully by giving him a special position so that his plan to restore the "throne" will be "impossible."[105] But Amos Yong states that due to his disabilities Mephibosheth is not fit for the throne.[106] How then can we expect any threat from Mephibosheth to David? Moreover, if David ever sensed such threat he could have ignored or easily killed Mephibosheth. But Rod Thompson asserts that David's words help us to understand his "desire" and the "character" of his administration.[107] The main emphasis is on the word "kindness" (חֶסֶד) and it is the key word of the covenant. Rod Thompson asserts that Mephibosheth is disabled because of

102 Geoffrey David Miller, "Attitudes Towards Dogs in Ancient Israel: A Reassessment" *Journal of the Study of the Old Testament 32*, no. 4 (2008): 488.

103 Deuel, "God's Story of Disability, 85.

104 Rod Thomson, "Mephi Bosheth at the table: A High Point in Davidic Kingship-2 Samuel 9:1-13, 145.

105 Christopher D. Rouse, "Scripture and the Disabled: Redeeming Mephibosheth's Identity" *Journal of Pentecostal Theology* 17 (2008): 190.

106 Yong, *The Bible, Disability and The Church*, 33.

107 Thomson, "MephiBosheth at the table: A High Point in Davidic Kingship-2 Samuel 9:1-13", 146.

covenant cursing to Saul and his family.[108] Rod Thompson further states that "David's embrace of covenantal kindness has overcome covenantal cursing."[109] It implies that Mephibosheth's disability is due to sin since his restoration is based on covenantal kindness.

However, though kindness towards the disabled is evident in the covenant, the text here is not explicit about the reason for Mephiboshth's disability. What the text makes clear is David's intention in showing kindness for Jonathan's sake (2 Sam. 9:1). David's desire to show kindness appears three times in 2 Samuel 9:1, 3, and 7, which set the climax of this text. It indicates that the narrator has emphasized kindness as a strong motive behind David bringing Mephibosheth to his table. Rod Thompson asserts that covenantal kindness is shown among humans with each other due to "reciprocal commitment to faithful love." The text makes clear that the secret behind David's kindness towards Mephibosheth is his intention to covey special regard to Jonathan his friend. In 1 Sam. 20:1-23 Jonathan made David continue to show his kindness towards his family and finally made a covenant with David. Jeremy Schipper asserts that David's action of kindness is nothing but the "faithful expression" of his commitment to his friend Jonathan.[110] At this point David is remembering the goodness of Jonathan and wants to do something for his sake.

What is really significant is the attitude shown towards the disabled rather than to find out the reason for disabilities. The fact is the perspective of God and man towards disabilities is not negative. What comes out strongly is a picture of God's kingdom in David's rule where kindness is shown towards the disabled. So, in this text also the connection between sin and physical disability has not been highlighted.

---

108 Thomson, "MephiBosheth at the table: A High Point in Davidic Kingship-2 Samuel 9:1-13 ", 150.

109 Thomson, "Mephi Bosheth at the table: A High Point in Davidic Kingship-2 Samuel 9:1-13 ", 151.

110 Jeremy Schipper, *Disability Studies and The Hebrew Bible* (New York: T&T Clark, 2006), 41.

2.4. Conclusion

In this chapter, I have considered the relationship between sin and the human body to find out whether physical disabilities are related to sin according to the Old Testament. Firstly, keeping the focus on the praiseworthy bodies of the Old Testament, the function of the protagonist in the narratives was carefully observed through the case studies of Rachel, Saul and Samson. The findings revealed that though each protagonist had admirable physical beauty or extraordinary ability, the effect of sin was very much evident in their character, conduct and integrity. Moreover, having a praiseworthy body shows neither the approval of God nor is it a criterion for being useful to God. Secondly, the perspective of the Old Testament towards the disabled was seen by studying three fundamental texts: Leviticus 21:17-23; Exodus 4:10-12; 2 Samuel 9:1-13. The study of these text has shown that God is not negative toward the disabled. Having a disability shows neither the disapproval nor the punishment of God. Rather he himself takes the responsibility and credit for disabled people and assures his own presence with them. In fact, he is sovereign in designing the faculties of every human body for accomplishing his purpose. Hence, stating disability is due to sin would be absolutely misleading. However, sin affects both able and disabled people, and a disability is not the result of any special sin. We must accept the fact that God has created each one with different abilities and his creative act goes beyond human ability. Just because someone is abler than others does not mean he/she is more righteous nor because someone is disabled does that mean he/she is a great sinner. Having discovered this, we will now look at the understanding of the church concerning the relationship between sin and disabilities down through the centuries, in the next chapter.

Chapter 3

HISTORICAL PERSPECTIVES OF DISABILITIES AND SIN IN CHRISTIANITY

3.1. Introduction

Our attitude towards disabilities has not simply emerged out of a vacuum. It has been associated with the strong tradition of the past. Having discovered the biblical perspective of disabilities and sin it is significant to study the historical perspective of disabilities in Christianity. This will not only help us to understand the past but also prompt us to meet the contemporary challenges. Looking at historical treatment towards disabilities in Christianity will help us to see the foundation of our attitude towards disabilities. Generally, the Christian faith has a long tradition of showing compassion towards the needy, the sick, the unfortunate and the disabled. However, due to the influence of the society and culture, the interpretation of the Scripture sometimes has been given an unexpected twist. The aim in this chapter is not just to gain information from the historical facts but to see their perspectives comprehensively so as to find whether there is a connection between disabilities and sin. This endeavor will cover three different periods: Ancient Church History from AD 30-AD 590, Medieval Church History from AD 590-AD 1517 and Modern Church History from AD 1517- to the present time.

3.2. Ancient Church History: AD 30-AD 590

In this section, our study will concentrate on the different perspectives and views of the ancient church about disability and find out whether sin behind disabilities is predominant factor.

Firstly, we will consider the influence of the Hebrew Bible in the ancient church. A. Brook Blanks and J. Smith assert that though ancient Christianity received fundamental principles from "Jewish roots" to deal with the "social and political ends" yet its perspective towards disability is significantly different.[111] They further assert that disabilities in ancient Christianity are not seen as "punishment" from God or "God's wrath", but as a means to display divine "message, mercy and power."[112] But Samuel N. Kabue asserts that in "Judeo-Christian culture", though "children with disabilities" were not put to death, yet it has been interpreted as "punishment for sin", "as loss", and "as something that illustrates human tragedy."[113] The genuine concern at this point is to know the basis for such interpretation. The Old Testament describes disabilities in many different ways and in many different contexts. The fact is there is no single unity of thought toward disabilities running throughout the Old Testament. What is clear is the fact that disability is something for which God takes complete control and credit to himself. Nowhere in the Old Testament is disability seen exclusively to be the result of any special sin, or

111 Blanks and Smith, "Multiculturalism, Religion and Disability: Implications for special Education Practitioners," 298.

112 Blanks and Smith, "Multiculturalism, Religion and Disability: Implications for special education Practitioners, 298.

113 Samuel N. Kabue, "Church and Society's Response to Disability: Historical and Sociological Perspective" *in Doing Theology from Disability Perspective: A Theological Resource Book on Disability 2011,* ed. Wati Longchar and Gordon Cowans (Philippines: The Association for Theological Education in South East Asia, 2011),120.

considered as loss, or human tragedy. No doubt, it is generally believed that all have sinned and all are affected by sin. God created the beautiful creation, including man and woman, with proper order. Sin has affected the whole creation and as a result the order of God's creation has been distorted. That disabilities only exist due to any specific sin other than the original sin is a wrong interpretation of the Scripture. It is crucial to remember that though the "assumption" of logical connection in the covenant in terms of obedience and disobedience and the possible effect of parents' sin upon their descendants in the Torah helps us to understand the relationship between "sin and disability", yet latter "in the post exilic period" we get clear indication from the prophets that God would not count the sin of parents upon their descendants (Ezek. 18:2-4 and Jer. 31:29-30).[114] Therefore, disabilities because of any particular or even greater sin would not be an acceptable interpretation. Andrus asserts that disability due to sin "was not always held and promoted" by the early church.[115] It is significant to note that the focus of "early church fathers" was not so much on "earthly circumstances or situations" but on "knowing Jesus" from whom "true life" comes.[116] Moreover, Arthur Jeyakumar asserts that according to "Judeo-Christian tradition" the term disability was not recognized as a separate group with special needs because it is not in the Bible.[117] The teaching that disabilities are the result of sin then was not the dominating concept in the early church.

Secondly, we will consider the treatment of the disabled in the early Christian community. Religion in any generation shapes the attitude and perspectives of human beings, just as Christianity did in a minor community of the first century. Paying special

---

114 Yong, *The Bible, Disability and the Church*, 51.

115 Andrus, "Theology and its Impact on People with Disability: An Ecclesiology Inclusive of People with a Disability" 147.

116 Andrus, "Theology and its Impact on People with Disability: An Ecclesiology Inclusive of People with a Disability", 147.

117 Arthur Jeyakumar, "The Early Church and Persons with Disability," *in Sprouts of Disability Theology 2012*, ed. Christopher Rajkumar (Nagpur: National Council of Churches in India, 2012), 44.

attention to the early Christians' lives, one can easily determine the influence of the interpretation of Scripture. The lives of the early Christians were mostly written between the first century and the middle of the second century. Jeyakumar asserts that in early Christians' writings such as "the Shepherd of Hermas, the Epistle of Barnabas, the Epistle of Clement, the Didache or the Teaching of the Twelve, the Epistle to Diognetus" though much about Christians' life has been mentioned, yet there are no apparent evidences of their attitude towards the disabled in terms of accepting and giving responsibility to them.[118] It indicates that in the early church disabilities was not a major issue. The complication of dealing with people with special needs did not rise as a deep concern in the fold of Christ. If it had been a major issue it would have deserved a special place in the writings of the early church. Jeykumar emphasizes such an attitude towards disability and states that early the Christian community was "inclusive" without any discrimination.[119]

Moreover, the evidences of the inclusiveness of the church can be clearly derived from the life of Origen, who had a disability, yet he was not rejected by the church. Instead he was given the privilege to "preach in churches", was "ordained as the priest" and was regarded as a "Great Biblical critic."[120] Didymus can be another example of someone who had a disability but "the Christian church honoured him by raising him to sainthood."[121] This was definitely a distinctly different treatment to the people with disabilities by the ancient Christian community from the non-Christian community who rejected and mistreated and even where "the babies with the disability were left to die by exposure" soon after they were born.[122] In spite of such treatment, if they still survived they lived "a miserable life of begging, prostitution,"

118 Jeyakumar, "The Early Church and Persons with Disability", 45.

119 Jeyakumar, "The Early Church and Persons with Disability", 45.

120 Jeyakumar, "The Early Church and Persons with Disability", 46.

121 Jeyakumar, "The Early Church and Persons with Disability", 46.

122 Deuel, "God's Story of Disability: The Unfolding Plan from Genesis to Revelation," 83.

and being "treated as outcasts."[123] Emphasizing God's love and care for the people with disability, the people of God "differed considerably" from their neighbors, in how they treated toward people with disability.[124] It indicates that the early Christian community was inclusive even in addressing the needs of people with disabilities. They did not ignore and condemn people with disability and did not associate their disabilities with sin.

Thirdly, we will consider the point of view of the early church fathers. A. Arumai Durai asserts that though early church fathers considered that disability is a curse due to "some sin" or "bad habit" yet "monasteries and schools of thought took care" of the people with disabilities.[125] They were not condemned or ignored but special concern was extended to them. "Polycarp of Smyrna (AD 69-156)" gave importance to "charity" for the people with disabilities "as a means of one's salvation"[126] Early church father Didymus while writing a commentary on Job emphasized that "the evil, suffering, and hardship that Job went through are under God's control in order to work out salvation."[127] It seems the early church fathers raised their voices that people with disabilities are not so because of any specific sin of theirs but they fall under God's sovereign plan and purpose. St. Basil pleads with the church to have deep concern for the needy in serving Christ.[128] St. Augustine the most influential person in contributing to the doctrine of the church, emphasized the "equality of all in the eyes of God" and was convinced that "fulfillment" of the

123 Deuel, "God's Story of Disability: The Unfolding Plan from Genesis to Revelation", 83.

124 Deuel, "God's Story of Disability: The Unfolding Plan from Genesis to Revelation", 83.

125 A. Arumai Durai, "The Church and the Otherwise-abled: A Historical Overview" in Embracing the Inclusive Community: A Disability Perspective 2010, ed. A. Wati Longchar and R. Christopher Rajkumar (Bangalore: BTESSC/SATHRI, NCCI &SCEPTRE, 2010), 22.

126 Durai, "The Church and the Otherwise-abled: A Historical Overview", 22.

127 Andrus, "Theology and its Impact on People with Disability: An Ecclesiology Inclusive of People with a Disability" 148.

128 Durai, "The Church and the Otherwise-abled: A Historical Overview", 22.

image of God in the "disabled" will be "in heaven."[129] He further encouraged that to assist people with disabilities was "as a cause for the salvation for the charitable."[130] Considering all these views of church fathers we understand that the voices of the early church fathers were notabsolutely negative, especially in connecting sin with disability. They rather emphasized God's sovereign hand behind it.

In keeping with this, early Christians were also more influenced by the apostles' lives of submission to the LORD. Nancy Eiesland asserts that an act of willingness to submit to "divine test" of a righteous person has always been considered as an ideal and admirable act.[131] God in his sovereign plan allows disability to the "righteous", and takes them through a most challenging and difficult period of time to be "purified and perfected."[132] Submission instead of grumbling is encouraged in the midst of disability for the greater benefits. Undergoing painful distress of "disability" in this life is only for a short period of time andwill bring a "heavenly reward" in the end.[133] The act of submission also helps in strengthening the faith. Andrus asserts that Didymus one of the early church fathers, a disciple of Origen, in his commentary on Job mentions that God allows painful struggles in the Christian life in order to strengthen the faith.[134] Submission was encouraged to gain an outstanding level of faith. Based on the argument of Didymus, Andrus further states that in the early church disability is not considered as a consequence of sin, but it was viewed "as a way to align one's life with the

---

129 Durai, "The Church and the Otherwise-abled: A Historical Overview", 22.

130 Durai, "The Church and the Otherwise-abled: A Historical Overview", 23.

131 Nancy Eiesland, "Encountering the Disabled God" *PMLA* 120, no. 2 (Mar., 2005): 585.

132 Eiesland, "Encountering the Disabled God" 585.

133 Eiesland, "Encountering the Disabled God" 585.

134 David Andrus, "A Theological Evaluation of Disability", *Missio Apostolica* 18, no. 2 (2010): 125.

savior"[135] The life the Savior was all about a life of submission to the heavenly Father.

As for the origin of the disability, one perspective of the ancient Church was that disabilities were the work of the devil. Nicole Kelley asserts some of the early Christian texts propose that demons can cause diseases.[136] According to the interpretation of the majority of Christian authors in most cases, epilepsy is considered to be "the work of the evil spirits"[137] Almut Caspary asserts Tertulian also believed that disability is due to an attack by the devil.[138] He implies that behind disabilities the hand of demons is very active. Moreover, this particular ideology continued even into the medieval period of Church history. In fact in medieval Christianity many disabled children were "tortured, rejected and even killed to ban Satan", because people "accused" disabled children of having connections "with Satan."[139] This perspective and treatment of ancient and even medieval Christianity towards disability clearly reveals that disability had a strong association with the devil. At the stretch of such perspective, the association of any specific sin of a person with disabilities is far away. Though sin is strongly connected to the devil, yet the devil has its own reasons to cause someone to be disabled. Job for example suffered not because of his own sin. He was an upright person in the eyes of God (Job 1:1).

Meanwhile in considering disabilities, what it means to be human was a crucial issue in the early church. It was significant

---

135 Andrus, "A Theological Evaluation of Disability", 125.

136 Nicole Kelley, "The punishment of the Body was Apparent in the Torment of the Human Body: Epilepsy in Ancient Christianity" *in Disability Studies and Biblical Literature 2011*, ed. Candida R. Moss and Jeremy Schipper (United States: Palgrave Macmillan, 2011), 211.

137 Kelley, "The punishment of the Body was Apparent in the Torment of the Human Body", 211.

138 Almut Caspary, "The Patristic Era: Early Christian Attitudes Toward the Disfigured Outcast," *in Disability in the Christian Tradition: A Reader 2012*, ed. Brain Brock and John Swinton (Grand Rapids: William B. Eerdmans Publishing Company, 2012), 29.

139 Durai, "The Church and the Otherwise-abled: A Historical Overview", 23.

to see the difference between man as the image of God and man as disabled. The emphatic point is that down through the centuries "the Churches have never acknowledged that persons with disabilities are created in the image of God."[140] It seems like any form of disability becomes sufficient ground to consider whether a person is human or not. Beates asserts that there is not much "direct reference to people with disability" found in "early literature", but while addressing disabilities attention was focused on image of God.[141] Leaders of early church "Irenaeus (ca. AD 115-200)", "Clement (ca. AD 150-215)", "Athanasius (ca. AD 296-373)" saw the difference between image, which refers to the rational nature of man, not lost at the fall, and likeness, which refers to moral nature, lost at the fall.[142] It indicates that whether it may be about the rational ormoral nature of man, ultimately the essence of the image of God remains in the immaterial part of the man. This helps us to understand that people with disabilities are the image of God.

Investigation from ancient Christianity revealed that sin behind disability was not the predominant factor. They were an inclusive community, showing God's love and care to disabled people. The nature of their inclusiveness was demonstrated in the church where people with disabilities were not only accepted, but also got the opportunity to be ordained for religious duties. In fact, some of them were raised even to the privilege of sainthood. The early church fathers emphasized God's sovereign act behind disability and developed an attitude of compassion and concern towards people with disabilities. Influenced by the apostles, the early church community regarded submission to God as a commendable act in the midst of disability. With regard to the origin of the disability, the sin of a person has not been stressed but the devil was blamed. Though they wrestled concerning the image

140 Longchar, "Culture, Sin, suffering and disability in Society", 180.

141 Beates, *Disability and The Gospel: How God Uses Our Brokenness to Display His Grace*, 86.

142 Beates, *Disability and The Gospel: How God Uses Our Brokenness to Display His Grace*, 89.

of God and disabilities, yet the disabled person was acknowledged as bearing the image of God.

3.3. Medieval Church History: AD 590-AD 1517

Although, the perspectives of the medieval Christianity concerning disability contain some of the same views as ancient Christianity, yet medieval Christianity offers some different and unique ideas.

Medieval Christianity holds disabilities as a punishment from God due to sin. The influence of Judeo-Christian tradition on sin and disability had already formed a stigma by this time. Yet "this was not the only interpretation which was widespread."[143] It indicates that medieval Christianity also believed that there was a connection between sin and disability. But Elaine Ledgerwood states that though there is a strong "historical connection" between sin and disabilities from "Judeo-Christian tradition", yet in observing brief biographies of the early and medieval saints, it was "questioned" in the medieval Christianity.[144] This suggests that disability due to sin is not the only interpretation which existed throughout the medieval church history. As in the ancient church history, disability was interpreted in many different ways, so also in the medieval church history.

Firstly, we look at some of the disabled people in the medieval period who have enjoyed the privileged status of sainthood. The "biographies" of the medieval "saints" reveal that they had disabilities.[145] Being saints, they made a tremendous impact in the lives of the medieval people, even though they had disabilities. In the eyes of Christians, they were considered very pious and holy, not sinners. Observing the lives of the disabled saints "disability" was considered "as a method of divine refinement."[146] Prov.

143 Cusack, "Graciosi: Medieval Christian Attitudes to Disability", 418.

144 Ledgerwood, "Saint not Sinners: An Investigation into the "Positive" Constructions of Disability by the Historical Church, 85.

145 Ledgerwood, "Saint not Sinners: An Investigation into the "Positive" Constructions of Disability by the Historical Church" 85.

146 Ledgerwood, "Saint not Sinners: An Investigation into the "Positive" Constructions of Disability by the Historical Church", 94.

3.12 can be the best example to show the "connection between disability and refinement."[147] Hannah Skoda, emphasizing the physical suffering of disabilities states that disability showed the "spiritual purification and a closer relationship to God" in the thirteenth century.[148] It indicates that physical pain opens the door of possibility to know deeper spiritual truth. The disabled person has potential to get closer to God by getting rid of the distractions of a worldly life. The important thing has to do with the person not being distracted by trying to make the most of this world. Indeed, it is true how people focus their attention in accomplishing much in this world and neglect their relationship with God. It also gives the opportunity to have immense spiritual benefits of imitating Christ.[149]

Besides that, disability enables a person to enter into such a state of physical pain and brokenness, which Christ already entered and removed the curse of sin. Taking the exemplary life of Francis of Assisi, a very famous saint of the medieval Christianity, Scoot Wells equates the disability of Francis "with the suffering of the living Christ" and "his endurance" of disability demonstrates a very exclusive "intense devotion, compassion and humility" in following the "footsteps" of Jesus.[150] It gives a clear indication that disability is not condemned, ignored or rejected by the medieval society linking it to sin. It was rather raised to a certain point of exalted status and privilege which can make an effective impact in the lives of the people.

---

147 Ledgerwood, "Saint not Sinners: An Investigation into the "Positive" Constructions of Disability by the Historical Church", 94.

148 Hannah Skoda, "Representation of Disability in the Thirteenth-Century Miracles de Saint Louis" *in Disability in the Middle ages: Reconsideration and Reverberation 2010*, ed. Joshua R. Eyler (Great Britain: MPG books Groups, 2010), 54.

149 Skoda, "Representation of Disability in the Thirteenth-Century Miracles de Saint Louis", 66.

150 Scoot Wells, "The Examplary Blindness of Francis of Assisi", *in Disability in the Middle ages: Reconsideration and Reverberation 2010*, ed. Joshua R. Eyler (Great Britain: MPG books Groups, 2010), 72.

Secondly, another significant perspective which the medieval Christians strongly held was that a person with disability receives special grace from God. Carole M. Cusack asserts that most of the medieval Christians considered people with disabilities to have had "special gifts" and that they were privileged to receive the grace of God in their lives.[151] Moreover, sometimes God also "demonstrates" his power and glory by healing disability.[152] On the one hand a person with disabilities receives the grace of God and on the other hand God's name is glorified. It indicates that disability was not seen as a loss, lack or tragedy, but the individual was looked upon as a privileged person who would experience God's grace. Disability becomes a channel through which God displays his grace. Ascetic life during the medieval period was considered as the highest form of religious acts and God's touching at the point of disease causes someone to achieve inspiring moral standards.[153] Disability in such a case was not considered as something negative, but set as an example of pious living for the medieval Christian community.

Thirdly, medieval Christianity believed that disability gives a message of warning and judgment to the able people. Observing the lives of the early and medieval saints, Ledgerwood is convinced of the fact that disability brings a judgment to normal people.[154] Reynolds asserts that disability reveals the value and attitude of each and everyone of the community.[155] It appears then that disability exists neither because of any wrong doing nor due to anyone's fault, but to judge the normal people. People with disability do suffer physically and mentally. But much more than that they suffer by the attitude of the society. Social stigma and prejudices become a real cause of their intense affliction. The great

---

151 Cusack, "Graciosi: Medieval Christian Attitudes to Disability", 414.

152 Deuel, "God's Story of Disability: The Unfolding Plan from Genesis to Revelation", 85.

153 Cusack, "Graciosi: Medieval Christian Attitudes to Disability", 415.

154 Ledgerwood, "Saint not Sinners: An Investigation into the "Positive" Constructions of Disability by the Historical Church", 96.

155 Thomas E. Reynolds, "The Cult of Normalcy", 27.

suffering of the people with disability comes from unintended inclination of the ablest people.[156] Disability has no connection to sin of the past or present, but the biases and preconceived opinions of able society are like a standard where the attitudes of normal people are clearly reflected. The attitude of the societies towards the disabled will determine the judgment they will face by God.

Our discoveries from medieval Christianity disclosed that though there was a connection between sin and disability, yet this was not the only interpretation. People with disability enjoyed the exalted status and honour of being saints in the medieval period. They inspired people by their life of pain and struggle, and demonstrated what it means to follow the steps of Christ. For them the state of disability opened the door of opportunity to know deeper spiritual truth and get a closer relationship with God. Medieval Christians also believed that the disabled situation of a person became a means by which God's special grace was manifested while at the same time God's name was glorified. Moreover, medieval Christians also believed that disabled situation of a person brought a judgment to normal people where their values and attitudes were revealed.

3.4. Modern Church History: AD 1517-Present Day

Modern church history begins with the great reformation of the 16th century. For a perspective of disability from the reformation period we take the examples of Martin Luther and John Calvin.

Martin Luther's (AD 1483-AD 1546) responses are two-fold toward the challenging perspectives of disability. A. Brooke Blanks and J. David Smith assert that Luther's view "about drowning children with disability" because they are not really "human children", but are "incarnations of the devil."[157] Moreover, Beates quotes Paul Althaus and confirms that for Luther the abnormally formed children were "not created by God but made

156 Yong, *The Bible, Disability and the Church*,12.

157 Blanks and Smith, "Multiculturalism, Religion and Disability: Implications for Special Education Practitioners", 298.

by the devil."[158] But this perspective of Martin Luther was not based on the Scripture, but was what he simply believed.[159] Stefan Heuser asserts that Luther's understanding apparently reflects not only the "medieval superstition" but also shows "contemporary responses to disability."[160] This perspective of Luther is based on "his assumption" that a disabled child is not from man but born of the devil and "killing the child" would mean "fighting" against the "devil."[161] His primary endeavor is to create a separate between "human beings and the devil's children not between normal and disabled beings."[162] It is significant to note that though Luther linked the origin of disability of infants to the devil, yet he was not explicit in connecting the sin of the person with disability. Based on his view, anintelligent guess of anyone could be that Martin Luther was quite negative towards disability, since he associated it with the devil.

However, Luther is very positive towards people with disability and encouraged others to show compassion towards them. Benjamin S. Wall brings Luther's understanding of disability from Stephen Heuser as he highlights a very unique perspective, that touching people in their need was a clear demonstration of one's commitment to "divine call to faithful exploration of God's will."[163] It shows a spirit of submission to divine mission.

---

158 Beates, *Disability and The Gospel: How God Uses Our Brokenness to Display His Grace*, 92.

159 Blanks and Smith, "Multiculturalism, Religion and Disability: Implications for Special Education Practitioners", 298.

160 Stefan Heuser, "The Human Condition as Seen from the Cross: Luther and Disability" *in Disability in the Christian Tradition: A Reader, 2012*, ed. Brain Brock and John Swinton, (Grand Rapids: William B. Eerdmans Publishing Company, 2012), 186.

161 Heuser, "The Human Condition as Seen from the Cross: Luther and Disability", 187.

162 Heuser, "The Human Condition as Seen from the Cross: Luther and Disability", 187.

163 Benjamin S. Wall, "Disability in Christian Tradition: A Reader Theological Contributions to Disability Course" *Ethics in Brief* 19, no. 2 (Autumn 2013): np.

Luther saw disability through positive eyes and "provides constructive ways" to deal with it.[164] Luther stood for the people with disability and "integrated them into worship."[165] He was also deeply concerned for the people with "disabilities" and the issue to "participate in the sacraments" of the church for them was strongly "addressed" and "defended" "in his treaties of 1520 of holy mass."[166] He emphasized that people affected by disabilities "deserve the same thing that we do."[167] It suggests that for Luther, though they have their own limitation and challenges, yet they stand on the same platform with able people while worshiping and expressing the true devotion to God. No discrimination should be practiced in the church. In this way Luther's perspective actually provides constructive encouragement to meet the challenges of disability.

Meanwhile, John Calvin (AD 1509–AD 1564), who was known for his development of theology in the second generation of the Protestant reformation, does not directly address disability.[168] But his perspectives and insight on disability can be productively drawn from the vast sources and the creative writings he has contributed to Christianity. Thus, by observing the evidences from his work we may come to know what he may have thought about disability. Calvin's view on disability can be drawn from his understanding of the image of God. "In his *Institutes of the Christian Religion*" though he accepted the traditional concept that the image of God primarily remained in the "immaterial aspect" of man, yet he still saw the man as a whole and it includes the physical aspects.[169] According to Calvin "the entire being was

164 Wall, "Disability in Christian Tradition, np.

165 Durai, "The Church and the Otherwise-abled: A Historical Overview", 25.

166 Durai, "The Church and the Otherwise-abled: A Historical Overview", 25.

167 Durai, "The Church and the Otherwise-abled: A Historical Overview", 25.

168 Deborah Beth Creamer, Re-reading Calvin and disability, *Journal of Religion, Disability and Health* 17, no. 3 (2013): 282.

169 Beates, *Disability and The Gospel: How God Uses Our Brokenness to Display His Grace*, 92.

affected by the fall."[170] It indicated that disability was due to the fall and it had affected every one not just some people. Calvin would never agree that disability "limits" the image of God.[171] In addition to this, one of the profound teachings that John Calvin made clear was that "evil is allowed or even decreed by God" to accomplish the glory of God.[172] The implication from Calvin's understanding of evil is clear that disability is not due to sin, but God in his plan and wisdom has permitted it for His glory. It indicates that disability falls in the intention of God. This will be made clear further when we will bring out the implication from Calvin's doctrine of predestination. It would simply suggest that "God has predestined each of us to ability/disability."[173] If this is the case, then Calvin would not accept that disability was due to any specific sin. Rather, Calvin would stand for the fact that "all have sinned."[174] To Calvin it is "pointless" to know the reason for the disability, because God's action is beyond human understanding.[175] In such an understanding sin cannot be the strong reason behind disability. More significantly Calvin advocated that God himself stands for people with disabilities and appropriate response of the church is demanded.[176] Disabled people "like all people are of sacred worth."[177] There should not be any discrimination in the churches. This language of Calvin

---

170 Beates, *Disability and The Gospel: How God Uses Our Brokenness to Display His Grace*, 93.

171 Deborah Beth Creamer, "John Calvin and Disability" *in Disability in the Christian Tradition: A Reader, 2012,* ed. Brain Brock and John Swinton (Grand Rapids: William B. Eerdmans Publishing Company, 2012), 224.

172 Amos Yong, "Disability and the Love of Wisdom: Deforming, Re-forming and Per-forming Philosophy of Religion" *in Disability in Judaism, Christianity and Islam 2011*, ed. Darla Schumm and Michael Stoltzfus (New York: Palgrave Macmillan, 2011), 207.

173 Creamer, "John Calvin and Disability", 216.

174 Creamer, "John Calvin and Disability", 223.

175 Creamer, "John Calvin and Disability", 223.

176 Creamer, "John Calvin and Disability", 224.

177 Creamer, "John Calvin and Disability", 224.

strongly suggests that the Church ought to develop a culture of inclusion irrespective of disability. Everyone including a person with disability is part of the body of Christ.

Following the reformation period it is possible that modern Christians "amplified" the concept of disability and sin.[178] Stressing the "fall of man" and arrival of sin at that fall, disability was considered to be the result of sin.[179] Since God cannot be counted responsible for such an undesirable consequence, the blame for the "physical disability" goes to the "devil" who is the "source" of "sin and the evil."[180] It was further reinforced by "a strong message" of the "reformation" that "what is not of God is evil", which helped people to consider disability to be evil.[181] It implies that disability is the work of the devil not of God. As for the sound explanation of the reformation era, it is interesting to note that the disability is the result of sin committed by Adam in the garden. But the conclusion of this explanation is questionable. If this sin has affected the whole of humanity, then why do we see only some are affected by disabilities and not all? If due to sin the whole creation, including men, is affected not just the few, then only disability is the effect of original sin is not "necessarily correct" interpretation.[182] It indicates an idea that some aremore sinful than others. With this paradox to consider, we turn to survey views in the modern age.

---

178 Andrus, "Theology and its Impact on People with Disability: An Ecclesiology Inclusive of People with a Disability", 143.

179 Andrus, "Theology and its Impact on People with Disability: An Ecclesiology Inclusive of People with a Disability", 143.

180 Andrus, "Theology and its Impact on People with Disability: An Ecclesiology Inclusive of People with a Disability", 143.

181 Andrus, "Theology and its Impact on People with Disability: An Ecclesiology Inclusive of People with a Disability", 145.

182 Andrus, "Theology and its Impact on People with Disability: An Ecclesiology Inclusive of People with a Disability", 145.

3.5. Modern Construct of Disability

Jeyakumar asserts that Arne Fritzson and Samuel Kabue while interpreting disability, mean that "the term disability" is a construct of the modern Society in order to put disabled people into an organized group.[183] It was not the construct of Judeo-Christian tradition.[184] It helps us to understand that disability in the modern society is a real issue and people with disabilities need special care. So serving them would be more effective and efficient if they were organized. However, as mentioned above, disability was not an issue in the early Christians community since they were an inclusive community. The whole purpose to organize them was to serve themnot just to condemn or ignore them, considering their disability to be the result of sin.

In this section the whole focus will be on the perspective on disability according to the Christians from the nineteenth centuries until today. It is significant to note that earlier people with disabilities were a very minor portion of the society. But due to the advancement of medical technology, disabled people got some relief and survived from formerly fatal conditions.[185] It helps us to know the fact that there are more disability-affected people living in the world now than ever before. "It is said that 10% of the human population has some deformity or the other."[186] Historically they were condemned, ignored and marginalized in the Christian community. While dealing with the people with disabilities, there are two significant emerging issues in post reformation Christianity which will be considered–inclusion and exclusion.

The focus of the ongoing debate centers on the controversy whether to exclude or include people with disabilities in the church and society. Much of the concern has emerged when the church

183 Jeyakumar, "The Early Church and Persons with Disability", 44.

184 Jeyakumar, "The Early Church and Persons with Disability", 44.

185 Beates, *Disability and The Gospel: How God Uses Our Brokenness to Display His Grace*, 108.

186 Longchar, "Culture, Sin, Suffering and Disability in Society", 175.

encountered people with disabilities. Eiesland asserts that in the General Convention of the American Lutheran Church in 1986, the decision was made for not giving "ordination" to a physically disabled person.[187] Such announcement was done because the "implicit theology" of holiness code (Lev. 17-26) still continues in the "actions and attitudes" of today's church.[188] People with disabilities are still considered "unclean" and they deserve to be on the outskirts of the "community."[189] It clearly indicates the perspective of the modern church towards disability where a sense of discrimination is definitely revealed in their words and actions considering disability as a cause of impurity and which spoils the holiness of God. However, with the "initiative" of the World Council of Churches (WCC) "the Ecumenical Disability Advocates Network (EDAN)" was formed for dealing with the needs of people with disabilities.[190] The goal of this endeavor is to stand for and support "the inclusion, participation and active involvement of the persons with disabilities" in every aspect of life in the "church" and "society."[191] It is an attempt of modern Christianity to stand against the view that disability is due to sin and makes someone unworthy, by developing inclusive attitudes towards people with disabilities. But true inclusion still stands out as a great challenge in many churches.

Jayne Clapton asserts that though in the "western society Christian churches historically have been and contemporary are" very much in the forefront in working with people affected by disabilities, yet they have given "little attention" to the "historical

187 Eiesland, "Encountering the Disabled God" 585.

188 Eiesland, "Encountering the Disabled God" 585.

189 Eiesland, "Encountering the Disabled God" 585.

190 Samuel Kabue, "Ecumenical Disability Advocates Network (EDAN)" in Doing Theology from Disability Perspective: A Theological Resource Book on Disability 2011, ed. Wati Longchar and Gordon Cowans (Philippines: The Association for Theological Education in South East Asia, 2011), 72.

191 Kabue, "Ecumenical Disability Advocates Network (EDAN)", 72.

construction of exclusion."[192] "Biblical theological imperatives such as care, compassion, mercy support" have been extended towards people with disability with minimum "moral notions for the inclusion."[193] This culture of the Church has a "different" concept of inclusion in response to the complexity of the exclusion.[194] The helping attitude of the church also to some extent covers the exclusion dimension of the church, because they just feel pity for the disabled and helpless. But the real problem lies in accepting the person with a disability as a valuable person in the church. Henri J. M. Nouwen in his famous book *Adam* asserts that the personality and ability of a person to accomplish great things in life have become the criteria to be more acceptable in the world.[195] It is significant to note that "each one of us is unique, known by name, and loved by the one who fashioned us."[196]

While investigating the disability perspective of Modern Church history we observed the point of view of the reformers. Luther blamed the devil for the appearance of disability but did not emphasize the sin of the person behind disability. In fact, he encouraged people to have an attitude of compassion towards people with disabilities and integrated them into the worship of the Church. Calvin gave importance to the disabled by showing the plan and intention of God behind disability rather than the sin of the person. For him it was futile to know the reason behind disability since God's work goes beyond human understanding. Both Luther and Calvin emphasized there should not be any discrimination in the church. Next, the post-reformation period

---

192 Jayne Clapton, "Disability, Inclusion and the Christian Church: Practice, Paradox and Promise", *Disability and Rehabilitation* 19, no. 10 (1997): 420.

193 Clapton, "Disability, Inclusion and the Christian Church: Practice, Paradox and Promise", 420.

194 Clapton, "Disability, Inclusion and the Christian Church: Practice, Paradox and Promise", 421.

195 Henri J. M. Nouwen, *Adam: God's beloved* (New York: Orbis Books, 1997), 37.

196 Nouwen, *Adam: God's beloved* (New York: Orbis Books, 1997), 37.

considered the original sin of Adam and Eve as the real reason behind disability and gave importance to the fact that disability is not from God. But such conclusion was questionable. In the nineteenth century onwards the church has been struggling as whether or not to develop a culture of inclusion for the people with disabilities. They derive their norm from the Levitical code that disability makes someone impure, unclean and unworthy. However, steps are being taken by the World Council of the Churches to include people with disabilities in every aspect of Church life.

3.6. Conclusion

In this chapter, our focus was on the historical perspectives of Christianity towards disability. We attempted to study the relationship between disability and sin in the ancient, medieval and modern Christianity.

In ancient Christianity, we focused on the influence of the Hebrew Scriptures on the early church, the treatment of early Christians towards disabled people and the views of the early church fathers. It is clear that sin behind disability was not the predominant factor. The Christian Community in the early era demonstrated an inclusive culture towards disability and gave privileges to people with disabilities to serve even in the position of clergy. Some of them made an effective impact on people by becoming saints. Early church fathers were convinced that God's sovereign purpose was behind their disability and encouraged people to stand with the disabled in their complexity of life with many difficulties.

In medieval Christianity, though there was sometimes a link between sin and disability, that was not the only interpretation which prevailed and was not accepted by all. We gave our attention to lives of the medieval saints who had disability. They inspired people by demonstrating a closer and deeper relationship with God in the midst of their disability. Medieval Christians also held two unique perspectives; one emphasized the special grace of God for the people with disability because of their situation, whereas the other one gave importance to the judgment of the normal person because of his attitude towards disability.

In modern Christianity, we considered the views of the reformers. Both Luther and Calvin did not ignore people with disabilities because of sin. Luther blamed the devil, but Calvin gave credit to God's act and plan in terms of its origin. They emphasized that the church should integrate people with disabilities into worship and ministry. In the post-reformation period, though there was an effort being made to connect original sin to disability yet it remained a questionable effort. From the nineteenth century, onward the Christian community has struggled with the issue of exclusion and inclusion.

There have been a variety of ways disabilities have been perceived in the Christian tradition. People with disabilities are sometimes considered as sinners, while at other times they are called saints. Sometimes the condition of disability was seen as the punishment for their sinfulness, but it has also been seen as having hidden divine purpose in the sovereign will of God. At times people with disabilities have been ignored and rejected while at other times some they were considered to have a privileged status of keeping a very unique and unusual relationship with God. Sometimes it was seen as the work of the devil while at other times it was considered as the occasion where God's power and glory were manifested. The church at the best has seen disability as the object of charity. But, while people with disability were treated kindly in the churches in general, still there was discrimination. Having discovered that linking sin to disabilities was not the only view in the history of Christianity's treatment of the disabled, we will consider the Hindu concept of sin and disabilities in the next chapter.

Chapter 4

HINDU CONCEPT OF DISABILITIES AND SIN

4.1. Introduction

Having considered the biblical perspective and the historical perspective of sin and disabilities of Christianity, in this chapter we will turn our attention to study the Hindu concept of disabilities and sin and compare with the perspectives to the Old Testament.

Traditionally many Hindus give no regard to the persons with disabilities though some feel pity and compassion for the disabled. People also regret having such a child in their family and are highly ashamed of living in the midst of surrounding socio-cultural context of competition and aggressiveness to get success in the life. The attitude shown towards them does not give any hope or peace to the disabled and is quite discouraging and challenging to those who stand with them. Sometimes disabled children are shunned and abandoned at birth. Moreover, people with disability have been traditionally seen as inauspicious in the Indian societies. Indeed, it is crucial to know the reason behind such attitude towards disability in Hinduism. The chief concern therefore, in this chapter will be to make a comprehensive study of the rational basis for their attitude towards disability. In doing so special attention will be given to study the concept of sin and the law of *karma* according to Hinduism. Having done that we will consider next whether retribution in Deuteronomy can be considered a close Old Testament equivalent to the Hindu concept of *karma*.

4.2. Sin in Hinduism

In order to see the connection between sin and disability we must have a clear understanding of sin according to Hinduism. Generally, when we think of sorrow, suffering, immorality, pain and struggle in human life often sin comes to our mind. But Hinduism deals with all these realities of life quite differently. Nobody can deny the complex philosophy associated with it. There is diversity of opinions and views. It is indeed difficult to understand the concept of sin in Hinduism yet it remains very crucial for our study. We will look at the concept of sin according to the Hindu scriptures.

Viswanathan states that apart from "mythology" there is no scriptural support for "sin" in Hinduism.[197] It suggests that reference to sin is found only in the epic literature. *Mahabharata and Ramayana* are the two prominent epic writings in Hinduism. It is a well-known fact to Hindu people that *Krishna* who played a crucial role in *Mahabharata* was an *avatar* "(a god coming to earth literally in the flesh)"[198] of *Vishnu* the sustainer god of the universe. He came to the world with a definite purpose to destroy the sinners and save the righteous. The most popular verses of *Bhagvad Gita* 4:7-8 states:

> Yada yada hi dharmasya glanirbhavati bharata
> Abhythanamadharmasya tadatmanam srijamyaham

197 Viswanathan, *Am I a Hindu?* 287.

198 Alexandru Corneliu Arion, "The Essence of Hindu Doctrine and its Influence on Christianity in America and Europe." *International Journal of Orthodox Theolgy 6*, no. 4 (2014): 179.

Paritranaya sadhunang vinashay cha dushkritam
Dharmasangsthapanarthay sambhabami yuge yuge[199]

Following English meaning of the above two verses has been taken from the Swami Vivekananda quotes.

> Verse 7: *Yada* = when, *Yada* = when, *Hi* = indeed, *Dharmasya* = of religion/duty, *Glani*= decay, *Bhavati* = is, *Bharata*= O Bharata (name of Arjuna), *Abhuthanam* = rising up, *Adharmasya* = of sin/chaos (note, the word "Dharma" means "religion", "*adharma*" means "not religion" or something against religion.), *Tada* = Then, *Atmanam* = Myself, *Srijami*= Create ("Srijami" means "I create"), *Aham* = I[200]

> Verse 8: *Paritranay*= to protect/save, *Sadhunang* =of the good or good people, *Vinashay* = to destroy/for the destruction, *Cha* = And, *Dushkritam* = of the evil or evil-doers, *Dharma* = religion, *Sangsthapan* = to establish, *Arthay* = to/for the sake of, *Sambhabami* = I am born, *Yuge* = In age, *Yuge* = In age[201]

Above two verses essentially communicate when the righteousness is decayed and unrighteousness is exalted, then the sustainer god of the universe intervenes in destroying the wicked and protecting the good for the sake of righteousness. (Refer Appendix 1 for the commentary on *Bagavad Gita* 4:7-8 by

199 "Bhagavad Gita Chapter 4, Verse 7-8: Yada Yada Hi Dharmasya" *Swami Vivekananda Quotes*, Accessed on August 20, 2017, http://www.swamivivekanandaquotes.org/2014/05/bhagavad-gita-chapter-4-verse-7-8.html.

200 "Bhagavad Gita Chapter 4, Verse 7-8: Yada Yada Hi Dharmasya" *Swami Vivekananda Quotes*, Accessed on August 20, 2017, http://www.swamivivekanandaquotes.org/2014/05/bhagavad-gita-chapter-4-verse-7-8.html.

201 "Bhagavad Gita Chapter 4, Verse 7-8: Yada Yada Hi Dharmasya" *Swami Vivekananda Quotes*, Accessed on August 20, 2017, http://www.swamivivekanandaquotes.org/2014/05/bhagavad-gita-chapter-4-verse-7-8.html.

Swami Vivekananda) Alexandru Corneliu Arion asserts that the purpose of the *avatar* is to "set thing aright" whenever "evil" gets worse in earth and disturbs the "order of righteousness."[202] In this case, there is a clear reference to sin at the heart of the mission of *Krishna*. In the same way, *Rama* in *Ramayana* appeared to kill *Ravana* whose sinful act was intolerable. Gopal Chandra Bayen asserts that "*Vishnu* the sustainer god incarnated as the human *Rama* to defeat *Ravana.*"[203] In both *Mahabharata and Ramayana* the sin refers to wicked deeds. In addition to this,not only epic literature but also *Purana* talks about sin. Jagdhari Masih asserts that it is only *puranas* which have recognized the concept of sin using the terms "*Punya* (merit)" and "*Papa* (sin)."[204]

Other than epic literature and *puranas* there is no reference to sin in Hinduism. Paul Younger and Susanna Oommen Younger also assert that there is no "doctrine of sin" in Hindu system of thought.[205] It indicates that the *Vedic* literature, which is very fundamental and authoritative scripture in Hinduism and considered to be the direct revelation from God do not record the concept of sin. It sets a challenge for us to understand the concept of sin since the most fundamental scripture of Hinduism, *Veda,* does not recognize sin.

However, though in *Veda* the idea of sin is uncertain and there is no direct and detailed description of sin yet there are numbers of synonymous words used in *Rig Veda* which give a notion of sin. Some of the technical *Sanskrit* words found to "signify 'sin': *agas, enas* (offensce) *adhidroha, drugdha* (malicious, treacherous) *kilbsa, repas* (stain) *rina* (debt)" remind us about some sort of

202 Arion, "The Essence of Hindu Doctrine and its Influence on Christianity in America and Europe", 179.

203 Gopal Chandra Bayen, "Epic Ramayana: Sociological Thought, Culture and Ancient Indian Science" The International Journal of Social Science and Humanities Invention 1, No. 6 (2014): 486.

204 Jagdhari Masih, *The Role of Swami Chinmayananda in Revitalization of Hinduism and Reinterpretation of Christianity* (Calcutta: Punthi Pustak, 2000), 103.

205 Younger and Younger, *Hinduism* (Niles Illinois: Argus Communications, 1978), 36.

action which is bad.[206] Here we get an indication that bad work is sin. Apart from this S. Gopalan highlights another important dimension of action which is "comprehensive" and it adds desires which compel and motivate man towards actions of all kinds.[207] It is not just outward action which is more visible but even inward force which is also considered as action. So in *Rig Veda* all the thoughts and actions which are bad could be considered as sin.

Moreover, when we pay close attention to the word or concept that really do mean sin in Hindu context, especially in the people's usage, then we find they clearly connect to the action which is evil. We must remember that they may not be significant but they do exist and people often use them when they talk of sin. In *Sanskrit* language there are many words for sin which refer to actions of all kinds. *Papa* is the most frequently used word by the Hindu people when they see any evil acts, immoral action or any action that hurts others. The philosophy of *papa* as per Swami Chinmayananda is that *Papa* refers to any action which "leaves regrets", and a sense of "guilt' in our minds.[208]*Papa* or sin is basically all "destructive thoughts" and actions.[209]*Adharma* is yet another word mostly used by the people in their day-to-day lives. *Adharma* primarily means opposite of *dharma*. *Dharma* is a very complex term in Hinduism. It includes "religious law, right conduct, duty and social order."[210] *Dharma* then refers to righteous conduct in the religious and social aspects of life. *Adharma* is the violation of that righteous conduct. It suggests that *adharma* refers

206 Ram Gidoomal and Mike Fearon, *Karma 'n' Chips: The New Age of Asian Spirituality* (London: Wimbledon Publishing Company, 1988), 92.

207 S. Gopalan, *Hindu Social Philosophy* (New Delhi: Wiley Eastern Limited, 1979), 98.

208 Masih, *The Role of Swami Chinmayananda in Revitalization of Hinduism and Reinterpretation of Christianity*, 103.

209 Masih, *The Role of Swami Chinmayananda in Revitalization of Hinduism and Reinterpretation of Christianity*, 104.

210 Arion, "The Essence of Hindu Doctrine and its Influence on Christianity in America and Europe", 172.

to such actions which are not accepted in the religious and social life of the community.

While studying the concept of sin in Hinduism we drew our attention to the Hindu scriptures. We discovered that there is no concept of sin in *Veda* the most holy and authoritative scripture of Hinduism. We found that though there is no direct reference to sin found in Hinduism yet epic literature and *Purana* explicitly deal with sin. According to epic literature and *Purana* sin is nothing but all the actions and thoughts which are evil. Even while looking at the synonymous words from the *Rig Veda* we found that sin means evil actions. In popular uses also, people often consider bad and unrighteous work as sin.

4.3. Sin and the Law of *Karma*

Having considered various possibilities of the idea of sin in Hinduism, we will consider sin in connection with the law of *karma*. It is one of the most significant and the most popular doctrines strongly believed and exercised in Hinduism. For a long time, this belief has made a very profound influence on the lives of Hindus in India. The term *karma,* primarily, means action. It is a "noun-form" and has derived "from the root *kri* meaning to do or to make."[211] It includes actions of all kinds such as "mental, verbal, or physical."[212] So it covers a wide range of actions both seen and unseen, thoughts and actions. Generally, it is by such actions that we hurt or make someone happy, please or displease God, realize and feel our wrong doings or not. It is the law of *karma* which judges the *karma* or action of all kinds. The law of *karma* is the principle by which good deeds are rewarded and bad/sinful deeds are punished. It is difficult to imagine bad works without pondering upon sin in religious context. We get a clear indication of how the bad deeds includes the idea of sin.

In the meantime, it is worth directing our minds to the Hindu scriptures to know their essential views about *karma*. Yuvraj

---

211 Poulami Chakraborty, "The law of karma and Salvation", International Journal of Humanities and Social Science Studies 1, no. III (2014): 192.

212 Chakraborty, "The law of karma and Salvation", 192.

Krishan states in *Vedic* literature and especially in "Samhitas and Brahmanas" *karma* is to perform "any religious act or rite" to get a better future.[213] Clear indication is assured for the better future on the basis of the *Vedic* ritual work. It helps us to understand that if no ritual work is performed than it is considered as bad *karma* and ultimately it will bring a very dark future. But it does not make the future clear in this present life or in subsequent life after death. Usually, when Hindu talks about future they refer to next birth. We get a clear picture that present performance can make a considerable amount of impact in one's future. Good works will bring a better future but bad work will bring a dark future. A bad work in this case is not performing the religious acts which actually plays the role of sin which will promise the upcoming worse future. This indicates that sinful work can bring an unpleasant future in life.

Moreover, *karma* in *Upanishads*, refers on one hand, to the moral law of "good and evil" and on the other hand to "bondage leading to transmigration and rebirth."[214] The reference to the moral law of right and wrong gives a clear idea of sin in which disability is a state of bondage. Without the concept of sin, it is hard to imagine the moral standard of right and wrong. According to *Upanishads* it is quite important to realize that the whole focus is to be free from the bondage by the work. The elements that can cause someone bondage gives a clear picture of sin. The bondage refers to the state of being slave which is often understood as the effect of sin.

In addition to this, it is good to observe Yuvraj's quotation from the famous teaching of *Bhagavad Gita* 2.47 "*Karmanye va adhikaraste ma phalesu kadacana*" meaning just do the work and expect no outcome from it.[215] Here the two key words (karmanya) *karma* or action and (phalesu) *Phala* or result are right at the center of our focus. This teaching of *Bhagavad Gita* can be better

213 Yuvraj Krishan, *The Doctrine of Karma* (Delhi: Motilal Banarashidass Publishers Private Limited, 1997), 4.

214 Krishan, *The Doctrine of Karma*, 17.

215 Krishan, *The doctrine of Karma,* 113.

understood in the light of the principle of *karma*. It puts the emphasis on the work and suggests that human expectation should be away from the fruits of the work. But it still does not deny the importance of the results or the fruits based on the work. This is the way good work in Christianity is also performed. The benefit may happen but the doer should not use it as his motivation. The point is that whether you expect fruit or not, fruits of the work are inevitable. This principle of *Gita* also falls under the principle of *karma*. Whenever a Hindus talk about the result of the work, they mostly refer to past sin. When someone does good work, he gets free from the bondage and ultimately, he will be united with the *Paramatman*. At that point he will get his reward, end his cycle of rebirth and be free from the result or fruits of sin. Therefore, often people in Hinduism link the present consequences with the sin of the past. In this way *Gita* provides an idea of sin for which a person ultimately bears the consequences as fruits of his work.

Having looked at the concept of the law of *karma*, we will consider sin in connection with the perspective of *Maya* in Hinduism. There is a strong connection between the law of *karma*, sin and *Maya*. The concept of *Maya* directly addresses sin in Hinduism. According to Viswanathan "we all sin or do *Karmas* because of ignorance."[216] The lack of ability to "discern right and wrong" is called *Maya* in Hinduism.[217] Sankara a well-known philosopher of Hinduism used this word *Maya* to explain that "*Brahman* alone is real", "everything else is *Maya*" and "*Maya* is false knowledge."[218] *Maya* blinds each and every person of the world and sin is committed with the false knowledge or ignorance. Due to lack of knowledge of reality one has to go through rebirth several times, which will be considered later in this chapter. Alexandru Corneliu Arion asserts that by seeing "reality" through the path of "knowledge" one will be free from

216 Viswanathan, *Am a Hindu?* 287.

217 Viswanathan, *Am I a Hindu?* 289.

218 Viswanathan, *Am I a Hindu?* 290.

the cycles of rebirth.[219] Because true knowledge of reality will help solve all human problems, it means the knowledge of reality or the knowledge of *Brahman* will end the process of rebirth. If there is no rebirth, there is no disability. That suggests that true knowledge of reality will free the person from being born with disability or from any other situation of life.

The tricky and curious point is to know the fact that even the doer does not know what he is doing. But the doctrine of *karma* emphasizes on the work which is actually done "knowingly."[220] The emphasis of the principle of *karma* is on work done intentionally. No one will escape from the outcome of such intentional work.[221] We get a clear reference that in the doctrine of *karma* deliberate work will bring the results that the doer deserves, whereas *Maya* promotes that a person does sin due to ignorance. It seems the concept of *Maya* contradicts the nature of work the law of *karma* signifies. Even though it talks about sin and explains the reason behind sin yet we must remember that *karma* is not sin. It is the principle by which both good and sinful deeds get their appropriate reward. However, it is significant to know at this point that mostly when Hinduism talks about *karma* the usage is in the negative sense. This is so popularly at any rate. When we understand sin in Hinduism connecting to the law of *karma* we are clear that there is a punishment for the sinful work done intentionally and the soul of a person enters into a cycle of rebirth and will be in bondage until it unites with *Paramatman*. This is why Hindus connect disability with the sinful work of the previous birth.

We investigated that the *karma* in Vedic literature emphasized the ritual work which gives a symptom of sin. Ritual work is primarily an invocation to solve the human problem. Ritual in Hinduism includes series of actions to get rid of evil. Often people do *Homa* (Religious offering made into fire). It

219 Arion, "The Essence of Hindu Doctrine and its Influence on Christianity in America and Europe", 176.

220 M. Hiriyanna, *The Essentials of Indian Philosophy*, (London: George Allen & Unwin, 1949), 48.

221 Hiriyanna, *The Essentials of Indian Philosophy*, 48.

is the source of the fulfillment of all the desires for material prosperity and physical wellbeing. A better future is assured on the basis of this ritual work. The reference to evil clearly indicates the concept of sin. We also looked at the term sin in the *Sanskrit* language where we found that the word sin or *papa* refers to actions which are immoral, evil and leave a sense of guilt in mind. Both outward actions and inward thoughts hurt and destroy others. *Adhrma* is another synonymous word for sin which is a violation of the religious law and conduct in the society. There is a punishment for *papa* and *adhrma* in the law of *karma.* It suggests that there is a strong connection between the *karma* and sin. *Karma* in *Upanishads* addressed the moral law of good and bad, and bondage. If a person does something ethically wrong than he will enter the bondage as the punishment. It offers a strong ideology of sin. The principle of *Gita* also falls under the law of *karma* and brings the most deserving fruits to the doer though he should keep his expectation away from the fruits. Next the relationship among the *karma*, sin and *Maya* was given due attention. The principle of *Maya* directly teaches that we do sin because of ignorance. But the law of *karma* contradicts the teaching of *Maya*. Works done intentionally are very significant.

This suggests that the idea of sin is very much found in the ideology of *karma.* It is the law of *karma* which relates to the present consequences with the sinful acts of the past birth. It is at this point people associate disability with sin assuming that disability is due to the sinful work of the past life. Now let us consider the relationship between the law of *karma* and disability.

4.4. The Law of *Karma* and Disability

Having studied the sin and the law of *karma* in Hinduism now we will focus on the connection between *karma* and disability, since the previous deeds have tremendous effect on present status of a person. O. P. Joshi asserts that the mystery of "suffering" and the "inequalities" which we see "among men in the world" are explained by the law of *karma*.[222] It suggests that people born with an able body or with disability are not just by accident but have been determined by the principle of *karma*. Viswanathan states that "the law of *karma*" gives knowledge and explanation about sin by the principle of "cause and effect."[223] It is the law of *karma* that promotes the idea of cause and effect. That is to say "wherever there is a cause, there is an effect."[224] So sin (*Papa*) is the cause and result (*phala*) is the effect. There is then a clear indication of disability having connection with *Karma* because the law of *karma* connects the two. It is indeed significant to discover the way *karma* functions and relates to disability.

Firstly, in order to understand the relationship of *karma* and disability we must consider the concept of *samsara*. *Samsara* is the transmigration of the soul depending on the deeds done in the previous birth directed by the law of *karma*. The law of *karma* and the concept of *samsara* give reasons for the differences we see among the men. *Samsara* helps us to understand the dispensation of retribution. It is a very complex phenomena of living beings since it deals with the transmigration of the souls and yet remains very central to the belief of people in Hinduism. Millions of Indians Hindu strongly abide by this concept as the reasonable means to establish harmony and order in their past, present and future life. The way Arvind Sharma has defined *Samsara* is nothing but "the process of undergoing rebirths" regularly.[225] Rebirth indicates that the death of the person is not the end of the soul. The soul will take another body and be reborn. It is generally accepted that the "soul" continues to "live" in "another life" going through a

---

222 O. P. Joshi, *Introduction to Hinduism*, (New Delhi: Preach Publications), 175.

223 Viswanathan, *Am I a Hindu?*287.

224 Masih, *The Role of Swami Chinmayananda in Revitalization of Hinduism and Reinterpretation of Christianity*, 17.

225 Arvind Sharma, *Classical Hindu Thought: An Introduction* (New Delhi: Oxford University Press, 2000), 94.

cycle of birth.[226] Actions of the previous birth are "attached to the soul", which play a significant role in determining the journey of the soul.[227] According to the law of *karma* since soul must pay the wages of *karma* of the past life, its returning to the work is nominated.[228] It then becomes necessary for a person to take birth several times in this process of principle. More surprising is the fact that the "process" of *samsara* is "without a beginning and an end."[229] It clearly indicates that everyone in this life is set to pay the wages of the past life. In such cases, disability has the purpose to pay the wages of past life.

Secondly, to get the reasonable explanation of why a person is born with disability let us pay attention to the heart of the law of *karma* and rebirth. We must know the fact that it is during the age of *Upanishad* where the law of *Karma* was meaningfully developed and connected to the idea of rebirth.[230] Since it was developed during the age of "*Upanishad*" it is highly philosophical and considered to be the most classical to Hindus. Masih believes that there is a strong relationship between *Karma* and rebirth.[231] As "one sows, so he reaps", the person who performs the action gets the result.[232] This is the most fundamental principle of the law of *karma* which governs the whole system of rebirth. "Every action produces its necessary result and every

---

226 Ram Gidoomal and Mike Fearon, *Karma 'n' Chips: The New Age of Asian Spirituality*, 89.

227 Viswanathan, *Am I a Hindu?* 140.

228 Solange Lemaitre, *Hinduism*, trans. John Fransis Brown (New York: Hawthorn Books Publishers, 1959), 74.

229 Sharma, *Classical Hindu Thought*, 94.

230 Masih, *The Role of Swami Chinmayananda in Revitalization of Hinduism and Reinterpretation of Christianity*, 17.

231 Masih, *The Role of Swami Chinmayananda in Revitalization of Hinduism and Reinterpretation of Christianity*, 19.

232 Masih, *The Role of Swami Chinmayananda in Revitalization of Hinduism and Reinterpretation of Christianity*, 19.

cause produces an effect."[233] As per this principle all are born in this world because of their past deeds and their rebirth will take place again on the basis of work of present life. Present conditions and unique circumstances of a person are the consequences of his past deeds. There is no accident or even coincidences involved in it. It indicates that a person is born with disability due to his sinful work of past life. The differences we see in the lives of the people with regard to their "classes or physical mental abilities" are due to their works of present as well as past life.[234] Classes here refers to the caste system and physical mental abilities refers to the disability. Sarah M. Whitman also asserts that mental and physical hardship of a person in this present life is considered to be "part of the unfolding *karma*."[235] It is the result of the improper actions "(mental, verbal, or physical)" of the past as well as present life.[236] The crucial point is, disability is not regarded as the "punishment but as a natural consequence of the moral law" in reaction to the actions of the past.[237] In this case the law of *karma* plays a vital role. God is not involved in judging the act and determining the subsequent consequences.

Thirdly, it is even more surprising to know that nobody is responsible for the work except the one who is actively involved in the work. A person's present status is neither accidental nor is fate involved in this complex. But the performer is absolutely responsible for his own future because he intentionally commits sin. People often associate the sin of family members behind disability or any tragedy that they encounter unexpectedly. It is profound to remember that, "the soul continues" to carry the burden of *karma* being born several times "until it exhausts all *karmas*" going through "pain and pleasure sensations in the body"

233 Arion, "The Essence of Hindu Doctrine and its Influence on Christianity in America and Europe," 181.

234 Arion, "The Essence of Hindu Doctrine and its Influence on Christianity in America and Europe," 182.

235 Whitman, "Pain and Suffering as Viewed by the Hindu Religion," 609.

236 Whitman, "Pain and Suffering as Viewed by the Hindu Religion," 609.

237 Whitman, "Pain and Suffering as Viewed by the Hindu Religion," 609.

to form a single identity with "*Paramatman*" in the end."[238] Painful struggle is "part" of human life and it will continue to remain till one gets "*moksha*" (salvation).[239] Robin Boyd asserts that "man as pre-existentand eternal soul, the atman" is caught by the "world of *Maya*" and automatically gets involved in the "*karma samsara*" and will be finally united with "*paramatman*."[240] It is the journey of a single atman, which is temporarily attached with the body, to be united with supreme atman. In such cases, whether rich or poor, with ability or disability, all are on a special mission to accomplish the chief aim of their lives. In Hinduism "pain and suffering" are even not exclusively considered as unpleasant or unwelcomed since some of the people chose suffering in their "spiritual" journey,[241] because it helps a person to be detached from the worldly pleasure and suffering to be united with *Paramtman*. The ascetic life for some of the people becomes a way to live. Physical suffering therefore is not always seen as negative and it gives meaning and purpose to life. But looking at the people who are struggling with disability because of some greater sin still remains in the minds and hearts of the people in Hinduism.

In addition to that, when the misfortune befalls a certain individual the blame goes neither to God nor to any family members and neighbors. No external force, person and even God is involved in it. So deep is the "conviction of some of the adequacy of *karma*" that people even do not "need to acknowledge the existence of God, conceived as the creator of the world and as its controlling Judge."[242] Ram Gidoomal and Mike Fearon also state the significant point of the *samsara* is that "God is out of the picture."[243] In *Bhagavad Gita* 5:14 "*Krishna says*" God is not responsible for performing the actions as well as determining

238 Viswanathan, *Am I a Hindu?*140.

239 Whitman, "Pain and Suffering as Viewed by the Hindu Religion," 609.

240 Robin Boyd, *An Introduction to Indian Christian Theology* (Delhi: ISPCK, 2000), 244.

241 Whitman, "Pain and Suffering as Viewed by the Hindu Religion," 609.

242 Hiriyanna, *The Essentials of Indian Philosophy*, 48.

243 Ram, *Karma 'n' Chips: The New Age of Asian spirituality*, 93.

the fruits of the actions.[244] He is not going to be involved in this situation either to improve or control. Each and every person is "ultimately responsible" for their own performances.[245] The problem lies beneath with regard to the judgment of the *Karma*. Since God is not in the picture, the judgment of *karma* is done either by the universal force or an automatic response, as a result of which the future destination is determined. Even the execution of the law of *karma* is a mystery and not known to us with regard to why a particular person deserves disability more than others.

Moreover, Ed. Biswanathan asserts that the destination of the soul after death will solely depend upon the *karma* of the past. Whether a person becomes "rich or poor", or is "born with disease" are due to the "actions" of the "previous life."[246] He further explains that it is the law of *karma* which gives the ideology of the differences we see around us.[247] Generally stating the fact that *karma* of the past life is responsible for the present situation is just not enough since we know nothing about our previous birth. Even the present situation will not give details reason for the consequences. As Jagdhari states, the reason people are not the same will never be made clear by the facts, events and actions of the present life.[248] Though there is a general logic of the law of *karma* yet it is not entirely possible to establish a cause and effect equation between past and present life. It seems like the law of *karma* is the ultimate authority behind the people born with disability though our lack of knowledge of the past life disadvantages us from fuller and detailed explanation. While the other dimension is that it is hard to accept that a poor person will remain in the same state. The status of man changes every now and then. He can be rich by his hard work in the present life

244 Viswanathan, *Am I a Hindu?* 150.

245 Arion, "The Essence of Hindu Doctrine and its Influence on Christianity in America and Europe", 181.

246 Viswanathan, *Am I a Hindu?* 140.

247 Viswanathan, *Am I a Hindu?* 141.

248 Masih, *The Role of Swami* Chinmayananda *in Revitalization of Hinduism and Reinterpretation of Christianity*, 17.

and a person born with diseases can be healed by the help of the advanced medical technology.

To sum up: first, while studying carefully the law of *karma* and disability we looked at the concept of *samsara*. We found that the soul of the person never dies. It continues its journey by going through a cycle of rebirth, taking the burden of souls. Every soul has a special mission to pay its wages. In such case disability is also in the special mission to clear the wages of the past life. Then the effort was made to see the reasonable explanation behind such philosophy. We discovered that our work becomes the only crucial factor behind the cycle of rebirth. Cause and effect is the principle which determines the whole course of actions.

Secondly, we found that a person is absolutely responsible for the consequences which were not by accident or fate. Family members, relatives or friends are not responsible for that. Even God is completely out of this picture. Since God is not involved in the law of *karma* exercising divine justice in determination of a soul's next birth is questionable.

Thirdly, it is important to know that in Hinduism pain and sufferings are not considered a punishment but they help people to experience a deep sense of meaning and purpose in the spiritual journey. But the mission of the soul is set to be united with *Paramatman* and that mission may involve suffering through disability.

It is clear that, though Hindus neither have a deep conviction about sin nor want to be called sinners yet the law of *karma* promotes the idea that there is an appropriate reward for righteous work and punishment for sinful work. They hold very strongly that all the situations of suffering or blessings of the present life are the consequences of the deeds of the past life. Disabilities or any struggles of life are therefore considered as cursing because of a person's bad work of the past. It is the law of *karma* which opens the way for the transmigration of a soul and leads it to be in bondage till it unites with the *Paramatman*. Though it is very difficult to relate our present life's struggle to the previous work since nobody is aware of what happened in the previous life yet the principle of *karma* connects the past sinful deeds with the present status of a person. It also promotes the idea that the doer is the one who is responsible for the consequences. Apart from the doer nobody is involved in the whole process of *karma*. So disability is not because of sin of the parents. Even God is not in the whole picture of the law of *karma*. The judgment therefore is automatic or exercised by the universal power as per the principle of *karma*. It is then clear that the law of *karma* clearly revealed the ideology of retribution in Hinduism. Having studied disability and the law of *karma* we will now look at retribution and disability in the Old Testament book of Deuteronomy.

4.5. Retribution and Disability in Deuteronomy

One of the emerging interests of Christians' in India is to find the beliefs of other religions that correspond to Christian doctrine. Giving importance to such a quest, in this section we will devote our sincere effort to study retribution and disability in Deuteronomy since the notion of divine retribution is basic in this book. The divine retribution in the law of *karma* has been understood negatively where the predominant factor is punishment due to sinful works of human beings. So, disability is seen as the consequence of previous deeds. It would be significant to know whether retribution in Deuteronomy emphasizes that ideology. Some key principles of divine retribution in Deuteronomy will be taken into consideration. In doing so we are developing a framework of sin-penalty as cause-effect, and that this work well in terms of parallel to Hinduism. This framework will not cover congenital disabilities to argue that these are the effect of a fallen world- this does not have any parallel within the concept of karma.

Firstly, Yahweh's relationship with his people is a significant part of retribution in Deuteronomy. In his relationship to man justice and jealously which are also very crucial in retribution, are integral. J. Gordon McConville asserts that Deuteronomy strongly holds the fact that God is a God of justice.[249] Bearing

249 J. Gordon McConville "Retribution in Deuteronomy: Theology and Ethics" *Interpretation: A journal of Bible and Theology* 63. No. 3 (2015): 288.

in mind the idea of "divine retribution in Deuteronomy", God standing against the evil is quite crucial.[250] In the context of manifold commandments in Deuteronomy, we can clearly see the maintenance of justice and jealousy of God. When we give our close attention to the Ten Commandments in Deuteronomy we see the jealousy and punishment of God for evil to the sons, grandsons, and great-grandsons have been declared (Deut. 5:9). In the context of the Ten Commandments, Deuteronomy dispenses the "essence of evil (awon) as idolatry"[251] Worshiping other gods than YAHWEH is something for which God is jealous. It is crucial to note the use of pronoun "I" and "you" which highlights the aspects of relationship. The "I"-"you" relationship is a very unique characteristic of the Ten Commandments.[252] It indicates that the jealousy of God has emerged out of this relationship. Divine acts of retribution in Deuteronomy are out of jealousy, and in divine action "justice" cannot be separated from God.[253] It seems that in the divine retribution of Deuteronomy God is at work as the God of justice. His action is not simply to justify the law code but to prove that He is a just God who loves His relationship with man. It gives a clear picture of God's involvement in the retribution. In fact, Stephen B Chapman asserts that retribution in the "Old Testament theology" emphasizes the interaction "between human action and divine response."[254] It suggests that sin behind disability is not the purpose of the retribution in Deuteronomy. Relationship takes priority over ignoring or condemning people with disabilities.

Moreover, God's involvement in retribution in Deuteronomy helps us to understand that the whole process is not simply operated by an impersonal force but by a just God who is a person. It is not regulated by an automatic system where God is not in the

250 McConville "Retribution in Deuteronomy: Theology and Ethics" 288.

251 McConville "Retribution in Deuteronomy: Theology and Ethics" 288.

252 Joze krasovec, "Is There a Doctrine of Collective Retribution in the Hebrew Bible" *Hebrew Union College Annual* 65 (1995): 53.

253 McConville "Retribution in Deuteronomy: Theology and Ethics" 289.

254 Stephen B. Chapman, *Reading the Bible as Witness: Divine Retribution in the Old Testament. Perspectives in Religious Studies* 31, no. 2 (2004):176.

picture. John G. Gammie is right in asserting that retribution in Deuteronomy is "personal, theocentric" through which Yahweh's active involvement of the past and present can be understood.[255] It is not operated by the philosophy or any impersonal principles, so that the consequences will not be determined by man but by God, who takes personal interest in human life. God is at the center of the retribution. If "retribution is a function of justice" than punishment will never be imposed by the impersonal system, but by the "person and nature of Yahweh."[256] It suggests that people with disability need a personal touch at the point of their struggle.

In Deuteronomy 6:4-5, the Israelites hear a call to love the Lord their God with all their hearts, with all their minds and with all their strength. In the following verses they are required to meditate on the commandments, teach them to their children, and tie them in their arms and foreheads. The significance of such requirements is mandatory because "a sense of rightness of things" remains very crucial at the back of all these commands in Deuteronomy.[257] God has given these commandments for man's good (Deut. 10:12-13). It is important to note that according to Deuteronomy "the rightness of things is the origin of the "righteousness" (sedaqa) in God." Unlike the focus of the retribution on punishments, in maintaining the justice in retribution God is seeking for man's good. Therefore, in the retribution in Deuteronomy divine justice can be considered as a strong pillar which strongly stands in the way of evil for the benefits of man. It encourages us to see the perspective of retribution where the goal is not on the penalties but the justice of God, and even in that justice, God wants to do what is good for man.

Secondly, divine faithfulness is an indispensable part of divine retribution. We will consider divine retribution from Deut. 7:9-10. Chapter 7 of Deuteronomy exclusively deals with the conquest of the Canaan. This section chiefly addresses how

255 John G. Gammie, "Theology of Retribution in the Book of Deuteronomy," *The Catholic Biblical Quarterly* 32.1 (1970): 9.

256 McConville "Retribution in Deuteronomy: Theology and Ethics", 293.

257 McConville "Retribution in Deuteronomy: Theology and Ethics", 289.

people of Israel should trust God, destroy the other nations and their cultic installations completely and know the basis for their election. Joze Krasovec asserts that "the retribution formula" is the attestation that there is nothing but God's choice as the basis of Israel's election out of rest of the people and he is "faithful" in keeping his "promises" which he gave to their "fathers."[258] God's faithfulness was demonstrated in the way he brought the people of Israel from the bondage of Egypt. At this point God and his faithfulness is the "basis" of his calling people to remain "faithful to their God" and therefore it is crucial to know the fact that there is a concept of "positive aspect" in the "divine retribution formula."[259] It indicates that God's faithfulness towards his people provides hope, comfort and victory in spite of retribution.

Thirdly, God's compassion is a significant part of Divine retribution in Deuteronomy. Often people relate God's anger and punishment in response to their sinful work when they think of retribution. There is a sense that receiving what is deserved is the appropriate act of God. However, retribution in Deuteronomy does not exclusively promote the idea of deserving as per the deeds of man.[260] Though God's anger is the appropriate response to the sinful work of man yet he did not get the "full measure of judgment" from God which he actually deserves.[261] God's dealing is completely different than the way man sees, understands and expects. It goes beyond human imagination. The song of Moses recorded in Deuteronomy 32 highlights the "judgment" of God in the setting of historical accounts "in which God has compassion" on Israelites.[262] As per the retribution formula the Israelites deserve nothing but utter destruction as a covenant breaking

258 Joze Krasovec, "Is There a Doctrine of Collective Retribution in the Hebrew Bible" *Hebrew Union College Annual* 65 (1995): 53.

259 Krasovec, "Is There a Doctrine of Collective Retribution in the Hebrew Bible", 53.

260 McConville "Retribution in Deuteronomy: Theology and Ethics" 291.

261 John G, Gammie "Theology of Retribution in the Book of Deuteronomy," *The Catholic Biblical Quarterly* 32.1 (1970), 10.

262 McConville "Retribution in Deuteronomy: Theology and Ethics", 291.

community. But the people of Israel did not get what they really deserved due to breaking the covenant; rather they were shown compassion by Yahweh. Beats referring to the phrase "I wound and I heal" from Deuteronomy 32:39 asserts that the "Judeo-Christian God" not only allows disability "in his sovereignty" but he also takes the responsibility to heal.[263] It is at this point we get a clear perspective of God "who is both the ultimate source and the ultimate solution."[264]

In Deuteronomy, there is a curse put on those who mislead a person with disability: Cursed is the one who misleads a blind person on the road. Then all the people will say, Amen (Deut. 27:18). It shows "God's love and care for the people with disabilities."[265] That does not mean the formula of blessing and cursing in the covenant has no ultimate effect and the way covenant conditions blessing and cursing might express a certain moral order. "God's compassion" is the underlying factor and plays a significant role in retribution in Deuteronomy.[266] Here we can clearly see God's compassion towards disability. The compassion of God plays a significant role in God's judgment and disability is not the punishment as per the sinful deeds. However, that does not mean the compassion of God is demonstrated in not allowing full measure of judgment. The judgment is so that repentance and restoration can take place. It is much more meaningful because it happens entirely within earthly life. This is revealed in Deut. 27-28.

While studying retribution and disability in Deuteronomy we discovered three significant facts. Firstly, we get a clear indication that disability in retribution in Deuteronomy is not considered as something negative in the sight of God. It is not even seen as

---

263 Beates, *Disability and The Gospel: How God Uses Our Brokenness to Display His Grace*, 32.

264 Beates, *Disability and The Gospel: How God Uses Our Brokenness to Display His Grace*, 32.

265 Deuel, "God's Story of Disability: The Unfolding Plan from Genesis to Revelation", 84.

266 McConville "Retribution in Deuteronomy: Theology and Ethics", 294.

the punishment because of sin, as per the principle of retribution. Secondly, God keeps disability very much within the context of relationship where he has assured his own faithfulness and compassion. He becomes the real source of encouragement for them. God's love, concern and care for the people with disability are truly evident in Deuteronomy. Thirdly, He encourages others to show the attitude of compassion towards people with disabilities by inserting laws. Since God himself stands with them, it provides a great hope for them. It shows that disabilities and the retribution in Deuteronomy is not seen as the consequence of sin. It is not even because of the anger of God. It is neither considered as a curse nor as a punishment from God.

However, the common assumption of retribution in Christian Theology is that disability is due to sin. In John 9:2, Jesus' disciples asked Him a question about whose sin was responsible for the blindness of man they encountered. It reveals the retribution mindset of Jewish people. But it is significant to note that in John 9:3, Jesus Himself liberated them from such an interpretation and perspectives of Jewish people. Jesus' response to the question of disciples was very direct and clear: "Neither this man nor his parents sinned." Having made this thing clear, Jesus gave a purpose behind the blindness. Jesus said, "He was born blind so that God's work might be revealed in him" (John 9:3). It indicates that disability is not a punishment because of sin in the past, rather a phenomenon where God's name will be glorified.

4.6. Comparison of the Law of *Karma* and Retribution in Deuteronomy

Having studied both the law of *karma* and retribution in Deuteronomy, we will do the comparison between the principle of *karma* and principle of retribution in Deuteronomy. Three significant comparisons will be shown below.

First, it is crucial to note that the focus of the law of *karma* is on sin and punishment. It emphasizes the fact that sinful works deserves appropriate punishment. According to the law of *karma* infliction of pain, sorrow and suffering is the automatic response to the sinful work a person did in his previous birth. But sin and punishment is not at the center of retribution in Deuteronomy. God keeps retribution very much within the context of his relationship with his people in Deuteronomy. Divine relationship with man is a very crucial part in the retribution in Deuteronomy. He brings blessings and cursing because he is jealous of his exclusive relationship with man. He does not like to see his people going after other gods. Even in judgment God opposes evil and seeks the benefit of his people. Man, society or any circumstances are not the center of retribution in Deuteronomy. But it is the relationship of God and man which remains at the heart of retribution.

Secondly, in the principle of *karma* God is not in the picture. God does not judge the *karma* of a person. The judgment is done either by an automatic principle or by an impersonal force which emphasize the consequences as per the deeds of the past. In such a case each individual is responsible for his present condition. Nobody else is responsible for that. A person's present status is the result of their past intentional deeds. But the judgment done in retribution in Deuteronomy is a by personal God. It is bound up with the character of God. Divine justice, love and compassion are integral parts of retribution. Even in exercising justice, God opposes the evil for the good of man.

Thirdly, the principle of *karma* emphasizes the cycle of rebirth. The soul of a person has to go through this cycle several times since salvation is not possible in one birth. According to the law of *karma* a soul will enter into *samsara* based on its deeds. It indicates that there is no restoration in this present life here on earth. But the retribution in Deuteronomy does not connect with the sinful deeds of the previous birth. In Deuteronomy God's judgment is done here in this earth and God's compassion is shown towards his people in order that they will repent and be restored in this present life. It is significant that both the law of *karma* and retribution in Deuteronomy oppose doing evil. But the law of *karma* links the present sinful deeds with the next birth whereas the retribution in Deuteronomy deals with everything here in this life. We found three significant points to note.

Firstly, God's relationship with man is an integral pillar of retribution in Deuteronomy. There is a unique function of the combination of divine jealousy and justice in maintaining the relationship with covenant people. God opposes the evil for the benefit of man and at the same time he gives priority to the relationship. Retribution in Deuteronomy is therefore not controlled by any impersonal force but by God. It helps us to understand that disability is seen within the context of divine relationship rather than in the context of punishment. God is at the center of the retribution not the punishment.

Secondly, a significant pillar of retribution in Deuteronomy is divine faithfulness. God's faithfulness in keeping his people is a predominant factor in spite of many difficulties. God has demonstrated his faithfulness in bringing people out of Egypt and that becomes fundamental in commanding the Israelites to walk in a right way. God's faithfulness provides a real strength to the people with disability.

Thirdly, God's compassion as a principle of retribution in Deuteronomy goes beyond expectation. We discovered that in God's judgment man does not get what he deserves as per his deeds. God in judging his covenant community demonstrated his compassion. He did not punish them as per their deeds. It is done so that people will repent and be restored. In the context of such a judgment of God disability is not as per the sins of the past but a cause for which God has compassion. On the whole retribution in Deuteronomy offers peace, comfort, promise and provision to the people with disability.

4.7. Conclusion

In studying the Hindu concept of sin and disability we looked at the sin and *karma* in Hinduism. We found that there is no direct concept of sin in the Veda which is the most authoritative scripture of Hinduism. According to Veda it is very difficult to connect disability with sin. However, we discovered that there is reference to sin in Hindu mythology and *purana* where sin is very much understood by the way of *karma*. Next, we gave our closer look to the law of *karma.* The law of *karma* is the principle where good works are rewarded and bad works are punished. We discovered that sin is very much connected to the idea of *karma* in Hinduism. The law of *karma* clearly provides explanation for disability through rebirth and *samsara.* It emphasizes that the disability is due to the *karma* of previous birth. It is seen as the punishment because of the sinful works of the previous birth. The law of *karma* is the ultimate judgment of all our actions. Therefore, the judgment is automatic or by impersonal force. God is not in the whole picture of the law of *karma.* Each and every soul has to go through a time of bondage and finally be united with the *Paramathman.* Disability due to the deeds of previous birth is a strong ideology of the law of karma.

However, retribution in Deuteronomy does not emphasize the same ideology as the law of *karma.* Disabilities in retribution in Deuteronomy are not considered as the consequences of sin. It is not seen as the punishment from God. God does not ignore and condemn people with disabilities. Divine love, justice, faithfulness and compassion remain at the center of retribution in Deuteronomy. God stands with the people with disabilities assuring his own presence and comfort. His faithfulness towards people with disabilities provides a real comfort for them to live in this earth.

Even though God dealing with the retribution in Deuteronomy is very differently where link between the deeds of the past and the present consequences of man is not a prominent factor, yet in popular Indian ideology disability is always caused by sin. It is because the *karma* ideology has tremendous influence upon the people of India including Christians. We will therefore study the popular culture of Indians towards disability in the next chapter.

Chapter 5

DISABILITIES AS VIEWED IN POPULAR HINDUISM AND INDIAN CHRISTIANITY

5.1. Introduction

In this chapter, we will focus on how people with disabilities are treated in Indian popular culture. In the previous chapter, we observed that sin is the real reason behind disabilities in Hinduism. According to the law of *karma* a person is born with disabilities due to the sin committed in a previous birth. While looking at the *samsara* we also discovered that disabilities appear as a consequence of sin, where the soul of a person sets out to pay the wages of the past going by through a cycle of rebirths. Having found this, we will now study the attitudes of Hindus towards disabilities in their popular culture. In order to do so we will attempt to consider the daily newspapers, magazines, You Tube videos, Bollywood movies and other relevant sources.

There are some significant reasons behind considering these media as a powerful source from which to draw inferences for the purpose of this thesis. First, it will help us to understand how the

Christian lay person reads and interprets Biblical texts. Havilah Dharamraj asserts that in hermeneutics, "interest has shifted to reception centered influence" on the interpretation of the text, that is the factor which influences the common reader in understanding his/her reading of the biblical text.[267] It is crucial to understand the influences on the mindset of the Indian Christian "man-in-the street." Thus considering popular media such as newspapers and movies will enable us to see how "public meaning triumphs over the particularities of the text's professed meaning."[268] Secondly, our consideration of popular media as an influence on hermeneutics factors in that we live in a period of advanced modern technology where digital influence has brought different form of literature, easily accessed by the people that "theology and theologizing have kept pace with each new expression of literature."[269] By "new expression(s) of literature" we mean, for example blog sites and You Tube videos. It is from these "bits and pieces" that the ordinary Christian "constructs their idea of the whole"[270] on any given real life issue such as human disabilities. Impressed by popular Indian culture, the Indian Christian reads the biblical texts influenced by his/her medium of instruction. So, in this chapter we will look at the law of *karma* vis-à-vis disabilities as depicted in popular culture, and from this we will extrapolate the possible influence of popular culture on the Indian Christian's reading of the biblical text on disabilities.

5.2. Newspaper Reports

Newspaper reports show that disabilities are associated with stigma. The February 2, 2014, article of Trudy Harris in The Hindu newspaper states that millions of Indians with disabilities are continually facing a real challenge of "discrimination and stigma"

267 Havilah Dharamraj, "Boldly Go: Tracking Trends in Comparative Literature" to be published in a forthcoming book, 3.

268 Dharamraj, "Boldly Go: Tracking Trends in Comparative Literature", 5.

269 Dharamraj, "Boldly Go: Tracking Trends in Comparative Literature", 6.

270 Dharamraj, "Boldly Go: Tracking Trends in Comparative Literature", 7.

in their daily lives continually.[271] More than 20 families came to Shanti Auluck's home to arrange a marriage with her daughter. But each family rejected marrying Auluck's daughter and turned back because she also had a son with "Down Syndrome."[272] They rejected the girl not because they found anything wrong in her but because her brother had disabilities. It gives a glimpse of how Indians look at people with disabilities.

In addition to this, on July 6, 2016, The Hindu brought to people's attention about the fact that "in October, 2013, in Union of India v. National Federation of the Blind the court had noted" people with disabilities were not able to continue their jobs because of "social and practical barriers."[273] Then we hear the story of Ira Singhal who was "not allowed to take the position in office" because of her "physical disability", even after passing her IAS exam.[274] We must acknowledge that all these social barriers have been formed in India by giving importance to Hindu ideology and, in the case of disabilities, the law of *karma* is in the forefront. The most significant reason for the "exclusion" of people with disabilities in Indian society is the strong hold of the law of *karma* as it promotes the disbelief disabilities are due to wrong deeds in a previous birth.[275]

---

271 Trudy Harris, "Stigma thrives for India's 60 million disabled" The Hindu, February 21, 2014. Accessed on 13.09.2017, https://www.dawn.com/news/1088491.

272 Trudy Harris, "Stigma thrives for India's 60 million disabled" The Hindu, February 21, 2014. Accessed on 13.09.2017, https://www.dawn.com/news/1088491.

273 "Disabled and Disheartened," The Hindu, July 06, 2016, Accessed on 14.09.2017, http://www.thehindu.com/opinion/editorial/Disabled-and-disheartened/ article14472708.ece.

274 Ayushi Anand "First Physically Challenged Women to Top IAS, Ira Singhal tells how her Disability was never an Excuse" *India Today*, May 9.2016. http://indiatoday.intoday.in/education/story/ias-topper-interview/1/663575.html.

275 Gayatri Ganesh, Chris Merin Varghese, "Mobility Devices for the Physically Disabled: A Story of Hope from Chhatisgarh, Central India", *Dharma Deepika* 20, No.1 (January-June 2016): 20.

Moreover, due to the law of *karma*, people with disabilities are considered inauspicious in Indian society.[276] Therefore, they have been stigmatized and oppressed. A mark of disgrace is strongly associated with disability-effected people in Indian society. On December 27, 2013, Monica Sarkar wrote an article for CNN stating that it is the strong influence of the law of *karma* and the "prejudice" that in Indian society people with disabilities are "at fault for their incapacity that affects their ability to live a normal life."[277] What really hinders acceptance of people with disabilities in Indian society is the attitude of people. This attitude has emerged out of the belief in the law of *karma* that disability is the result of wrong doing in the past life. They hold steadfastly to their belief that the sinful work of the past life is the root cause behind disabilities. Such a belief prompts people to think disabled people are the worst sinners and this may be one reason why they develop such negative attitudes towards disabilities. For example, on December 3, 2014 *Quartz India* published an article by Manu Balchandran clearly stated that Indians treat people with disabilities in such a "cruel and flawed" way that disability-affected people are considered "worse than animals."[278]

Another aspect of disabilities as reported in the newspaper shows that women with disabilities suffer a lot in India. On January 8, 2017, Hindustan Times highlighted the statement of Kolkota-based disability activist Shampa Sengupta. According to her, for a woman with disability, "the stigma" is "more pronounced."[279]

---

276 Gayatri Ganesh, "Mobility Devices for the Physically Disabled: A Story of Hope from Chhatisgarh, Central India", 20.

277 Monica Sarkar, "Disability in India: The Struggles of Infrastructure, Prejudice and Karma", CNN, December 27, 2013. http://edition.cnn.com/2013/12/27/world/asia/india-disability-challenges/index.html.

278 Manu Balachandran, "India Treats its Mentally Disabled Worse than Animals", Quartz India, December 3. 2014, https://qz.com/306299/india-treats-its-mentally-disabled-worse-than-animals/.

279 Poulomi Banerjee, "Disabled women not thought to be wife material by many", Hindustan Times, January 08, 2017, http://www.hindustantimes.com/india-news/disabled-women-not-thought-to-be-wife-material-by-many/story-QMqdQ4CSo43GQg5diavRGL.html.

Then on December 5, 2014, an article was published in Indian Express by Anuradha Mascarenhas where Kriti Sharma, a Human Rights Watch researcher reveals that "women and girls with a disability are dumped in institutions by their family members or police in part because the government is failing to provide appropriate support and services. Once they are locked up their lives are rife with isolation, fear and abuse with no hope of escape."[280] Next Anita Ghai, a disabled women asserts out of her experience that a woman with disabilities has no significant place in Indian society.[281] On July 27, 2017, we read in The Times of India that a 34-years-old wife from Jaipur, Rajasthan, was "abandoned by her husband" due to her disabilities and no help was assured assured by "the government" to her father on whom depended completely.[282] Again we see that women "whom have disabilities" are at times even "locked up, abused and kept" in impoverished conditions.[283] Recently, on July 4, 2017, The Hindu newspaper brought to our attention that "a 22-year-old mentally challenged women was allegedly raped by a 23-year-old in North Delhi Cashmere Gate on July 2."[284] Women already get treated worse than men because of the patriarchal structure which values

280 Anuradha Mascarenhas, "Women with disabilities Locked away, abused: HRW Report", Indian Express, December 05.2014. http://indianexpress.com/article/cities/pune/women-with-disabilities-locked-away-abused-hrw-report/.

281 Anita Ghai, "Disabled Women: An Excluded Agenda of Indian Feminism" *Hypatia* 17, No. 3, (Summer 2002): 49.

282 Rosamma Thomasl, "Sahariya Worried for Disabled Daughter, no Help from Government", The times of India City, July 27, 2017. http://timesofindia.indiatimes.com/city/jaipur/sahariya-worried-for-disabled-daughter-no-help-from-government/articleshow/59794570.cms.

283 Debra Killalea, "India's Shame: The Women 'Treated Worse than Animal' news.com au.Dec. 4, 2014, http://www.news.com.au/lifestyle/real life/true stories/indias-shame-the-women-treated-worse-than-animals/news-story/cb5e838172ee7aeb86a83354afb296d3.

284 Hemani Bhandari, "Mentally challenged women raped", The Hindu, July 4, 2017. http://www.thehindu.com/news/cities/Delhi/mentally-challenged-woman-raped/article19206569.ece.

the male. This less-valued female then becomes totally de-valued by disabilities.

If women suffer more than men in this area, disabled children even are more at risk from adults. Children with disabilities also go through very difficult times in India. The news came in Times of India on September, 10, 2016, that a 35-years-old mother from Jaipur, knowing the fact that her baby had "neurological problem", killed her own new born baby of day-old being worried that the child might develop physical "disabilities" at a later stage.[285] Her step to kill her own child clearly indicates that disabilities are not welcomed in the society. So, strong is the negative perspective of Indian society that a mother is even compelled to kill her own child. More recently, on August 13, 2017, a 26 years old woman of Coimbatore gave "poison" to her "7-years-old disabled son" and then committed suicide by taking "pesticide."[286] On 5 August, 2007, Times of India City brought to public attention a man from New Delhi, Dinesh, who frequently "committed unnatural sex" with a 14-years-old disabled boy.[287] Such reports demonstrate how vulnerable is the position of those afflicted.

Significant to our investigation of the relationship between the concept of *karma* and the condition of human disabilities, on February 07, 2017, In his article "Disabilities and the culture of violence" in The Hindu, Martand Jha states that those who are disabled at their birth have "committed some grave sin in their previous birth" which further causes development of an attitude

285 Ravishankar Bhujanga, "Mother Claims Murdered Child had Brain Disorder" *Times of India*, Sep. 10, 2016, http://timesofindia.indiatimes.com/city/jaipur/Mother-claims-murdered-child-had-brain-disorder/articleshow/54259889.cms.

286 "26-yr-old woman poisons disabled son kills herself, The times of India City, August 13, 2017. Accessed on 10.9.2017, http://timesofindia.indiatimes.com/city/coimbatore/26-yr-old-woman-poisons-disabled-son-kills-herself/articleshow/60039711.cms.

287 "Disabled boy's testimony sent sex offender to jail," The Times of India City, August 05, 2017, Accessed on 12.9.2017, http://timesofindia.indiatimes.com/city/delhi/disabled-boys-testimony-sends-sex-offender-to-jail/articleshow/59923083.cms.

of "discrimination and hatred" towards people with disabilities in the Indian culture.[288] This kind of attitude clearly reflects that India still firmly holds the stigma which has been handed down through the centuries. Such a stigma makes the going of people with disabilities very tough.

The attitudes of the general public are even by the government. On January 22, 2017, Virali Modi, a US citizen living in Mumbai, realizing the danger to disabled people traveling by Indian train wrote an open letter to the Prime Minister Narendra Modi and the Railway Minister Suresh Prabhu requesting them to provide an "efficient mode of public transport for disabled people in India." But this open letter was ignored by the Prime Minister Office (PMO)."[289] According to "2001 census", though there are "21.9 million people", even more are affected by disabilities in India, yet no effort is being taken by the government to deal with their physical and emotional needs.[290]

It appears that such attitudes of both the government and general public, in families and at the workplace, have been shaped and developed because of the ideology that disability is the punishment for sin of a previous birth. Families regard their disabled children as a curse and burden. Often people with disability have been linked with personal tragedy and left to suffer because the law of *karma* strongly emphasizes that their disability is the consequence of the wrong deeds done in the past birth. Nobody is seen to be responsible for that except the disabled

---

288 Martand Jha, "Disabilities and the culture of violence", The Hindu, February 7, 2017. Accessed on 13.09.2017, http://www.thehindu.com/todays-paper/tp-opinion/Disability-and-the-culture-of-violence/article17206805.ece.

289 Virendrasingh Ghunawat, "PMO ignored 'opened letter' and complained made by disabled girl, instead passed the buck to MEA", *India Today*, January 22, 2017. http://indiatoday.intoday.in/story/pmo-ignored-open-letter-and-complain-made-by-disabled-girl-instead-passed-the-buck-to-mea/1/863411.html.

290 Divya Shreedharan, "My body has also needs", The Hindu, May 09, 2015. http://www.thehindu.com/features/magazine/my-body-also-has-needs/article7184098.ece.

person. Throughout the years, people with disabilities have, therefore, been marginalized, oppressed and stigmatized.

5.3. Bollywood Movies

Next we will consider Bollywood movies, a very influential, powerful and accessible medium which reflects the popular culture of India. Hence, it becomes very significant to understand how disability has been portrayed in Indian Cinema. Indian films have manifested their attitude towards disabilities by the behavior and the language that the characters use to reveal their discrimination. To study this, we will take the Bollywood movie *Dosti,*[291] *Taare Zameen Par.*[292]

5.3.1. Dosti (1964)

Dosti (1964) communicates a strong ideology of how people with disabilities have been treated by the Indian community. It is a story about two friends Ramu and Mohan, one lame and the other blind who struggled in the Indian street to survive. Having been deserted by their families and preceded by series of unfortunate incidents in both of their lives, they accidentally meet each other in the street. Eventually they started their painful journey of meeting their bare necessities and fulfilling their dreams. At this point we see the treatment of able people towards them. They were discriminated against multiple ways in public places. First, in the street they were cheated and deceived by people. This movie shows a book store owner happy after deceiving them for money. Secondly, they were ignored and condemned by people, even by their own family members. The blind man's sister saw her own brother begging in the street and ignored him. Thirdly, people made fun of them in public places. They slept in a foot path where

291 Ban Bhatt, *Dosti*, Directed by Satyen Bose, performed by Sudhir Kumar Sawant, Sushil Kumar Somaya (1964, India: Tarachand Barjatya, Rajshri production,1964), Film.

292 Amole Gupte, *Tare Zameen Par,* Directed by Amir Khan, performed by Darsheel Safary, Amir Khan, (2007, India: Amir Khan Production, 2007), Film.

even an able person even tries to steal their hard-earned money. In such a context, the blind man appealed to the people in a song, requesting them to give their kind attention towards him because, he stated "I am just a man like you." and "I also reflect the same image of the creator who has created you all in his image." These statements reiterate the fact that the disabled are not considered on par with able persons and suggest that the disabled are thought of as somehow deficiently created.

5.3.2. Taare Zameen Par (2007)

Taare Zameen Par (2007) is a movie which highlights the disabilities of children. This movie basically encourages the idea that a child with disabilities can live up to his potential if parents and society give him special care. But while communicating this message, it explicitly shows us how disabilities are ignored and condemned by able people in Indian society. In this movie, a child with disabilities struggles in his family and in school. Nobody understood him in school because that is school for able people. Perhaps everyone is so preoccupied with the ability of the majority that they give no attention towards the one with disabilities. The head mistress of the school meets his parents and points out that he "has a problem" and "some children are very unfortunate." She explains that he is a child with special needs and that there is a different school for him. Even after her explanation, his father is not ready to accept that his child is abnormal. Then his father plans to send him to boarding school. Even in the boarding school the teachers' perspective towards disabilities is very negative. For them an abnormal, child with special needs has no future. Initially almost all the teachers condemn and ignore him. But in the boarding school he finds one teacher who understands his problems because he has gone through similar problems in the past. The description of disabled persons as "unfortunate" and "abnormal" can be understood as placing the blame for the disability on the disabled themselves, as if they have brought it upon themselves.

5.4. Quora and Blogs

Quora is question and answer internet site where people get direct and objective answers for any problems. In response to a question about why the attitudes of the Indians towards disability is very dismal, Shraddha J Agrawal first blames the "society" and states that the real reason behind such attitudes is the "old beliefs and superstitions which passed on to this generation from the previous generation."[293] It appears to refer to the principle of *karma* which has had tremendous influence upon the lives of the Indians down through the generations. The attitudes of people give a real challenge to disabilities-affected people to live in their communities. Virali Modi states along same lines that most Indians' "mentalities are crowded by the judgment" whenever they see people with disabilities.[294] It seems Modi refers to the principle of *karma*, as according to the law of *karma*, the righteous work of a previous birth gets a reward but the sinful work of the previous birth gets punishment. The evidences of the judgmental attitude of our society can be seen by noticing the attitude of a woman who saw a person with disabilities in the shopping mall and stated that "because of the sin of the previous birth he is going through disabilities"[295] Next Sai Prashad, in spite of having disabilities since his birth, studied technology in India as well as in America and out of his experience states that "my suffering is due to lack of infrastructure and ideology that relates disabilities with sin and fate in our country."[296] After conducting a survey "point of View"

293 Shraddha Agrawall, "The attitude towards disabled in India is very dismal. What do you think the problem is?" Quora, June 18, 2016, https://www.quora.com/The-attitude-towards-disabled-in-India-is-very-dismal-What-do-you-think-the-problem-is.

294 Virali Modi, "The attitude towards disabled in India is very dismal. What do you think the problem is?" Quora, June 13, 2016. 06.09.2017, https://www.quora.com/The-attitude-towards-disabled-in-India-is-very-dismal-What-do-you-think-the-problem-is.

295 Tube Buddies, "Documentary on Disability in India" You Tube video, 6:47, November 15, 2016, https://www.youtube.com/watch?v=nl3-K_3MkJQ.

296 Satyamev Jayate, "Satyamev Jayate S1I Episode 6 I Person with Disabilities I full Episode (Hindi)" You Tube Video, 1:04:30, June 9, 2012. https://www.

discovered the fact that, though misfortune of a person is not associated with disabilities yet being a disable in India is a biggest tragedy.[297] Such a statement clearly gives a picture of how people with disabilities have been treated in India.

5.5. Popular Christianity and Disabilities in India

As discovered above, popular Hindu culture reveals that general attitudes towards people with disabilities are significantly negative. People with disabilities are stigmatized and looked down on in the family and society, discriminated against in the workplace and ignored by the government. Bollywood movies and other media demonstrate inhuman attitudes and condemnation towards people with disabilities. Such attitudes of people towards disabilities in popular culture have been maintained because of the influence of the law of *karma* as it strongly connects sin with disabilities. As a result, people, whether consciously or unconsciously, make that connection. This is in contrast to the attitude Indian Christians should take. They should not connect sin with the disabilities or any kind of present sufferings, because, as we saw in the first chapter, the Old Testament does not link sin with disabilities. Though disabilities have been perceived in many different ways in the history of Christianity the fact is that sin does not the cause them.

Nevertheless, we see even Indian Christians who reveal the same attitudes towards disabilities as the Hindus. A good example may be seen in how some well-known Indian Christian preachers associate past sinful deeds with present consequences, sometimes using the teaching of the generational curse. Using these as sources we will demonstrate how the concept of *karma*, so prevalent in popular media, seems to have influenced Indian Christian thinking on disabilities.

---

youtube.com/watch?v=39SNcM99o4Q.

297 Point of View "Disability in India I Everyday Problems I Point of View, You Tube video,6:40, February 3, 2017, https://www.youtube.com/watch?v= qdxqDNWqb_E.

First, we will see how pastors are relating sin to sickness in their preaching. K Shyam Kishor is a pastor of Jesus Christ of Nazareth Ministries (JCNM), Hyderabad, in his preaching strongly implies from Mathew 8:17 that sickness and diseases are the result of sin.[298] Such teaching clearly links disabilities with the sin of the person. Next Father Joseph Edattu working with Divine Retreat Centre, (DRC), Kerala, makes a very explicit statement while preaching that a person gets sick because he remained involved in sinful habits in his good days.[299] This is another direct connection between sin and sickness. A very famous Malayalam pastor K. Joy of Indian Pentecostal Church (IPC), Delhi, states in his preaching that present suffering of the body is the result of living in deadly sins of the past and yesterdays.[300] In his lecture "Ultimate Teaching: Sick Body is Dangerous", Dr. Pillai, a spiritual scientist from southern India quotes from 1 Peter 2:24, "He himself bore our sins" and draws the direct implication that we sin due to ignorance and ultimately get sick.[301]

These examples clearly reveal that there are Christian in India who still hold that there is a cursing because of the sinful work and wrong deeds of the past generations. The Indian Christian mindset of some demonstrates very much the same ideology as the principle of *karma* in Hinduism. Christians actually should not perceive disabilities in this way. But some still abide by the belief that people have sickness because of the past sinful deeds done either by themselves or by their forefathers. In such cases, disabilities are seen as the consequences of sin.

---

298 Shubhsandeshtv, "Shyam Kishor I God's Will is to Heal Every one! I Part 1I09," You Tube Video, 28:34, September 11, 2015, https://www.youtube.com/watch?v=2SQHLUV41Es.

299 lovejesusdivine "Preaching by Fr. Joseph Edattu (English)" You Tube video, 9:15, April 18, 2013, https://www.youtube.com/watch?v=imFq2w4zfLo.

300 Christian sermons, "Sin-Part-1-Malayalam Christian Message by Pr K. Joy," You Tube video, 1:03.18 April 24, 2013, https://www.youtube.com/watch?v=rvAe-5Sn84k.

301 Pillai Center, "Ultimate teachings: Sick body is dangerous" You Tube video, 4:10, teaching, August 11, 2015. https://www.youtube.com/watch?v=6G0P5QkLp3Y.

Secondly, we will see how preaching connects sickness/ disability not just to sin but also to a curse-that is to continuing effect of past sin, which is the basis of the concept of *karma*. Indian Christians perceive suffering through persecution positively, because People suffer persecution for their faith. But sickness is not seen positively. Rather, as stated above, it has a strong connection with sin and is often referred to in terms of a curse. Pastor Santosh Prabhu from Adonai International Ministries, Bangalore, makes a very explicit statement in his preaching that "sickness" is the "result of curse."[302] Next M. K. Sundaram, pastor of Apostolic Christian Assembly (ACA), Chennai, also while preaching states that those who commit sin against a servant of God will face "a danger in life", "God's curse" will be upon them, and they have "no admission into the kingdom of God."[303] Along the same line, the late DGS Dhinakaran, founder of Jesus Calls ministry, Chennai, strongly stated as God's prophet that whoever commits sin against the servant of God is a cursed one.[304] Further some preachers connect present suffering to sin committed by the forebears of the one who suffers sickness. Zac Poonen, pastor of Christian Fellowship Church Bangalore, in his preaching explicitly mentions that some Christians believe even today that there is a "generational curse" because "some idols" were worshiped by their "great, great, great, great grandfather."[305] A very direct connection between sickness and *karmic* retribution comes from Pastor Brian Zahnd. In his preaching titled "Jesus vs. *Karma*" Pastor Brian Zahnd of Word of Life Church points

---

302 Adonai International Ministries Bangalore, "Pastor Santosh Prabhu-Jesus can turn Curses into Blessing, English & Kanada" You Tube video, 28:19, March 16, 2015, https://www.youtube.com/watch?v=orYGE3csAbE.

303 jeddy boy 03, "Sin of Foolishness P 2", You Tube video, 7:41, November 19, 2009, https://www.You Tube.com/watch?v=ezObHOOPUGc.

304 Prayer Mansion, "Warning to People Who Criticizes God's Servant-Bro. DGS. Dhinakaran" You Tube video, 5:25 July 1, 2013, https://www.youtube.com/watch?v=YqxaXX228xU.

305 SermonIndex.net "Why God Allows His Children to Suffer by Zac Poonem", You Tube Video, 58:08, March 19, 2011, https://www.youtube.com/watch?v=17Dc18Zkc_Q.

out that not only the Hindus and Buddhists link the past sin with the present suffering but also numbers of Christians claim that a person goes through present suffering because of "bad *karma*."[306] This teaching clearly reflects the teaching of the principle of *karma* which emphasizes definite punishment due to sinful work.

Thirdly, preachers become quite judgmental in delivering the message. The late DGS Dhinakaran, emphasizing judgment in one of his sermons, stated that "God is angry with the wicked every day."[307] This teaching closely resembles the teaching of the Gita that *Krishna* appeared as an *Avatar* to destroy the wicked. It gives a hint that God hates the wicked sinner. That becomes enough encouragement for Indian Christians to link sin with present suffering. Disabilities in this case are considered a clear manifestation of God's judgment upon the wicked. Apostle Ankur Narula, pastor of Church of Signs and Wonders, Punjab, emphatically states in his preaching that if someone commits sin then he "neither can ask great things nor can do great things."[308] It gives an indication that sin becomes the real cause for not getting great blessings, gifts and responsibilities from God. It is the language where sinner is absolutely ignored and condemned. This kind of teaching again reflects the cause and effect of the law of *karma*. This makes a sinners' life quite hopeless. Sin destroys the comfort, joy and peace of life.[309] Paul Dawson, founder of Miracle Healing Centre, Chennai, in his preaching states that sickness is the "work of the kingdom devil", a "curse" and if anybody is sick he is

306 Word of life Church, "Jesus vs. Karma I Pastor Brain Zahnd I Word of life church" You Tube video, 36:03, July 9, 2013, https://www.youtube.com/watch?v=vK3UOpir6SY.

307 Jesus Calls, "Forgiving sin (English-Hindi) -Bro. DGS. Dhinakaran", You Tube video, 9:44, November 12, 2016, https://www.youtube.com/watch?v=Gy0-ZyAdmUI.

308 God is One Only Jesus, "The Effect of sin (part 1) A sermon by Apostle Ankur Narula", You Tube video, 22:34 June 23, 2017, https://www.youtube.com/watch?v=-vKQFYksp2g.

309 Masihi Geet HD "Sin Destroys your Comfort But Forgiveness is from Jesus Only, Apostle Ankur Narula," You Tube video, 20:19, May 20, 2007, https://www.youtube.com/watch?v=DUb0xsKL7F8.

far away from the kingdom of God.[310] The implication here, even if implicit, is that, first, disability is the work of devil. Secondly, it is also considered as the curse. Thirdly, person with disability has no place in the kingdom of God. At this point we need to specify that we are extrapolating the sample to apply to disabilities from the sample that strongly connects sin and sicknesses.

5.6. Conclusion

While looking at Indian popular culture we investigated whether the law of *karma* has made any influence on the current Indian perception of disabilities. From the newspaper reports we discovered that a mark of disgrace has always been associated with people with disabilities. It has ultimately affected the lives of people with disabilities in the family, in society, and even in the workplace. They face a real challenge to work not only in the small-scale sector but also at the IAS level. People see them as unholy and treat them even worse than animals. Women with disabilities suffer a lot by being even more devalued in the male-dominated context. Children are abused and killed. Similarly, Bollywood movies show that people with disabilities are deficiently created and considered unfortunate and abnormal. In such a context, it is difficult for a disabled person to mingle with normal people. Along the same lines, websites such as Quora and You Tube show that the attitude towards people with disabilities is quite dismal. People with disabilities experience the judgmental mentalities of people in their day-to-day lives. Such kinds of attitudes are a representative reflection of their karmic ideology in which they are well rooted.

However, it is surprising that some Indian Christians also are influenced by the same kind of ideology as shown in their preaching and teaching. We discovered many Christian preachers in India who relate sin of the past with present sickness. They also further associate diseases with a generational curse. It indicates the

310 MIRACLEHEALING CENTRE, "How to Dominate Sickness and Disease", You Tube video,50:17, March 16, 2012, https://www.youtube.com/watch?v=hxU9ziYjX44.

belief that sin is the real reason behind disabilities. We also found that the preaching and teaching of some Indian Christians also emphasize the principle of cause and effect which is the core heart of the law of *karma*. That means sin is a cause and disabilities are the effect. Besides they become too judgmental in their preaching. They become too quick in judging certain acts and situations of people and make dogmatic statements out of their insights. All these aspects in their preaching reflect very much the same ideology of *karma* and retribution in Hinduism. Indian Christians who are influenced by such preaching also develop negative attitudes towards disabilities. It seems that Indian Christians are also influenced by the principle of *karma*. Therefore, it becomes easy for Indian Christians to believe that disabilities are due to sin.

CONCLUSION

In this book, we set out to study the perception of disabilities in the Old Testament and in Hinduism. Specifically, we desired to explore the connection between disabilities and sin, that is to see if disabilities are retribution for sin. In the second chapter, we studied selected Old Testament narratives of disabilities to see if disabilities were associated with a negative evaluation of the characters. Having done that, we gave due attention to the historical perspectives of disabilities in Christianity in the third chapter. Following this investigation, we studied the association Hinduism makes between disabilities and sin in the fourth chapter. Having found the fact that sin is the sole reason behind disabilities according to the principle of *karma* or retribution in Hinduism, we compared this idea with the principle of retribution in Deuteronomy in the Old Testament. Finally, to achieve the purpose of this study we considered Indian popular media which widely show the general Indian perceptions on sin and disabilities and then showed these perceptions to be part of Indian Christian thinking as well.

In the first chapter, "Old Testament perspective on disabilities and sin", we endeavored to discover whether disabilities in any way related to sin in the Old Testament. We looked at both praiseworthy bodies and disabled bodies in the Old Testament.

In the first section of this chapter we primarily focused on the narratives which considered praiseworthy bodies. Having found descriptions of the extraordinary beauty, strength and abilities of protagonist in the Old Testament, we picked up some of the key ones relevant to our study and made an earnest attempt to see whether on the one hand they were affected by sin in spite of being admirable for their praiseworthy bodies, and on the other hand whether their praiseworthy bodies become criteria to get the stamp of blessing from God. We tried to observe carefully the function of the protagonists within the narratives.

While considering the case study of Rachel from Genesis 29-30, we got a very clear picture of her extraordinary beauty compared to Leah. But in the context where women with children were honoured, Rachel suffered degradation and shame for being barren for quite a long period of time. As the narrative unfolded, the effect of sin was very much displayed in Rachel's character. She revealed her envious spirit because her sister Leah had children whereas she remained barren. In fact, the narrator makes clear that it was the Lord who opened the womb of Leah while Rachel remained childless (Gen. 29:31). Then she was even manipulative in introducing surrogacy as a means of getting children. It indicated that her praiseworthy appearance was not the criterion to get blessing from God; rather a clear picture of her sinful character comes through alongside her beauty.

In considering Saul's praiseworthy body, we focused on his physique, character and conduct. Saul's praiseworthy body is described in (1 Samuel. 9:2). He was a "good" (טוֹב) good young man as compared to other people of Israel. His personality appeared much praiseworthy and admirable when compared to others. The narrator makes it clear that he stood head and shoulder above everyone else (1 Sam. 10:23). Saul is described as choice and more handsome than any one in the land. In addition to his physical appearance, he seems very special because on many occasions he is described as the one chosen by God (1 Sam. 10:24, 24:10, 2 Sam. 1:14). However, the effect of sin is very much evident in his character and conduct. His sinful character compelled Saul to demonstrate sinful conduct. He displayed a life of disobedience to God. Even after disobeying God, he did not accept the blame and put the blame on others for his own weakness. He also exceeded his authority in performing sacrifices. He was very much controlled by his self and will. It demonstrates that Saul's praiseworthy body neither indicates piety nor becomes the criterion to get blessings from God.

Focusing on Judges 13-16 we discovered that Samson was known for his supernatural strength. From his birth account, we know that he was consecrated for special service to the LORD even before he was conceived. But the narrator explains that he dishonoured his parents, did not pay any serious attention to his Nazirite vows and broke them. He did whatever was pleasing to his eyes. In this way, he was so entangled with sin that he finally had to lose his own life. His progressive development in committing sin, has been clearly narrated.

Through the case studies of Rachel, Saul, and Samson we found that though the protagonist had most admirable physical beauty or extraordinary ability, the effect of the sin was very much evident in their character, conduct and poor integrity. Hence, as the narratives were unfolded, we could clearly see three significant things. Firstly, the reflection of their sinful attitude was exclusively seen in their dealings with others. Secondly, having admirable physical bodies did not necessarily ensure flawless moral conduct. Thirdly, physical beauty, strength, and abilities did not become the criteria to be useful to God. All this strongly indicates that having a praiseworthy body does not make someone free from the sin. Indirectly it also supports the explicit idea that sin is not the real reason behind disabilities because in these cases able bodies were very much entangled with sin.

Next, we observed the Old Testament perspective towards disability from three significant and fundamental texts: Leviticus 21:17-23; Exodus 4:10-12; 2 Samuel 9:1-13.

Leviticus 21:17-23 directly prohibits anyone having deformities from performing priestly activities at the altar. It seems at a superficial level that God is negative towards disabilities. But we saw that blemished priests were not completely banned from the priestly activities. The primary focus of this text then is not on discrimination against disabled priests. This text is primarily concerned with how Israel should be a pure representation of God. It therefore refers to the essential characteristics of the people who approach to the holy place. Moreover, we see God's concern for people with disabilities in the wider context of Leviticus (Lev. 19:14). So in the wider frame work of Leviticus, God is not negative towards disabilities. Furthermore, in this piece of text, sin is not seen as the real cause behind disabilities. While studying Exodus 4:10-12, we get an even clearer understanding of God's perspective towards disabilities. In this text Moses makes series of excuses when God calls him to his task. In one of his excuses he mentions that he is not a man of speech. God's answer in response to Moses' excuse offers wonderful perspectives towards disabilities (Exod. 4:11). We see that here God himself takes the responsibility for people having disabilities and uses them significantly. He is sovereign in allowing as well as keeping people with disabilities. Here again we don't see a link between sin and disabilities. In considering 2 Samuel 9:1-13 we discovered the attitudes of David towards Mephibosheth who became crippled in both feet. Here David showed kindness towards Mephibosheth in the time of his prosperity. Sin as the reason behind disabilities is not highlighted in this text, but rather David's intention in showing kindness for Jonathan's sake is the emphasis.

Thus, the study of all these texts shows three significant things. Firstly, God is not negative towards disabilities. Disabilities are seen neither as the punishment nor as the disapproval of God for sins. Secondly, it is crucial to know that God himself is sovereign in designing the whole structure of a human body for accomplishing his purpose. Disabilities then have a real meaning in the plan of God, since he will accomplish his purpose through them. Thirdly, God is the one who takes the responsibility of people having disabilities. He also encourages others, as seen in the case of David, to show their love and compassion towards disabilities-affected people. He assures his own presence and comfort to them. Therefore, based on these findings we can reasonably infer that sin is not the real cause behind disabilities according to the Old Testament.

Having been discovered that in the Old Testament disabilities are not seen as the consequences of sin, we looked at the historical perspective of the church concerning the relationship between sin and disabilities in the third chapter. In this chapter we investigated the historical perspective of disability from ancient Christianity until the present day.

Christians of the ancient church inherited principles and perspectives from the Hebrew Bible to deal with the multiple complications of society, including disabilities. But ancient Christianity offered significantly different perspectives as disabilities for them were neither explicitly seen as the punishment for the sin nor regarded as human tragedy due to God's wrath. Disabilities were rather considered as a means to demonstrate the message, power, and glory of God. The early church fathers focused more on knowing Jesus than on earthly circumstances. Being convinced of the fact that disabilities fall under the perfect plan and purpose of Sovereign God, they encouraged people to stand with the disabled in their daily struggles. Monasteries and schools were opened to meet the special needs of the people having disabilities. In fact, in the early church, disabilities were not a major issue because Christians were an inclusive community. They did not ignore, discriminate against or condemn people with disabilities, but rather emphasized God's love, care, and concern. Their writings also revealed there was no discrimination on the ground of disabilities. Besides that, the early Church also opened to people with disabilities the privilege to serve in the position of clergy where they influenced others by their teaching and preaching in the church. Though there was a disagreement about whether people with disabilities are counted as the image of God, our careful investigation revealed that they are. In addition to that, the lives of the early Christians were also influenced by the lives of the apostles which helped them to develop the culture of submission to God who allows disabilities to the righteous to purify their lives and strengthen their faith. Thus, in the ancient church, sin was not seen as the reason behind disabilities.

In medieval Christianity, the belief of some in a connection between sin and disabilities had formed a stigma, yet that was not the only interpretation nor was it widely accepted by all. We gave our attention to the biographies of the medieval saints who had disabilities. They made a tremendous impact upon people by their inspiring lives by demonstrating a closer and deeper relationship with God in the midst of their disabilities. The profound fact is that they were not considered sinful, but holy. Their lives became an example for the people to follow the footsteps of Christ. In fact, the suffering of people with disabilities was equated with the suffering of Christ. It enabled a person to experience the pain and brokenness Christ had already gone through. In this way disabled people were not ignored or condemned but raised to the most exalted state of honour by which they made an effective impact in the society.

In addition to that, medieval Christians held that people with disabilities were a privileged group who experienced divine grace in a special way. They were the channels and means by which God manifested his special grace. Besides that, the disabled also gave a warning message from God to the able people of society. It was in the light of disabilities the attitudes of normal people were tested. This kind of treatment from God helps us to understand that God is not negative towards disabilities. Rather they have a great meaning and value in the plan and purpose of God. They are not considered as the consequences of sin. Here again we found that sin as the real cause behind disabilities was not a dominate perspectives in medieval Church.

Next, while studying the perspective of the modern Christians we considered the view of the two influential reformers Martin Luther and John Calvin. Neither of them saw disability as the result of sin. Luther saw disabilities as the work of the devil and Calvin saw disabilities as the sovereign act and plan of God. They both emphasized that the church must be an inclusive community where disabled people have a place. There should not be discrimination on the ground of disabilities. They stood for and encouraged the integration of people with disabilities in worship and ministry. In the post-reformation period the connection between sin and disabilities was amplified stressing the arrival of sin at the fall of man as the due reason. But such a conclusion was questionable since sin has affected all, not just the people with disabilities. The issue of the exclusion or inclusion of people with disabilities have been a real challenge from the nineteenth century. Therefore, disabilities being due to sin is not the only interpretation through Church history. There are multiple ways disabilities have been treated in the Christian tradition. Sin behind disabilities has not been the predominant belief in the history of Christianity.

With this done, in the fourth chapter we studied the concept of sin and disabilities in Hinduism compared with the idea of retribution in Deuteronomy. We discovered that the most fundamental and authoritative scripture of Hinduism, the *Veda* does not mention sin. Since the *Veda* does not talk about sin, it becomes difficult to connect disabilities with sin in intellectual Hinduism. However, there is a clear reference to sin in Hindu mythology and the *Purana*. People also often talk about sin in their popular usage. So, in popular usage Hindu people connect sin with disabilities.

To understand the connection between sin and disabilities we studied the law of *karma*. It is the law of *karma* which gives a reasonable explanation of how sins of the past are connected with present disabilities. The law of *Karma* actually is the principle by which good deeds are rewarded and sinful deeds are punished. At this point we understood that disabilities are the punishment for past sinful works. All the deeds of a person are judged not by God but by an automatic principle or by an impersonal force. After the judgment by the law of *karma*, a person is reborn and enters into *samsara* as per the sinful deeds of the past. *Samsara* is the transmigration of the soul. The soul of a person has to go through the cycle of rebirth till it gets united with the *Paramatman*. It is impossible for a person to be united with *Paramatman* in one attempt and therefore it becomes mandatory for a soul to go through the cycle of rebirth. Another dimension is that each and every soul has to go through a time of bondage which might involve disabilities. So we investigated and found that disabilities due to the sinful deeds of the past life is the strong ideology of the law of *karma*. This is the way retribution according to Hinduism is understood and believed.

Following that, we studied retribution in Deuteronomy. Though there is retribution in Deuteronomy, it is quite different from the law of *karma*. We looked at some of the strong pillars of retribution in Deuteronomy. We discovered first, that God's relationship with his people was very much fundamental to retribution in Deuteronomy. While maintaining this wonderful relationship he also exercised his justice. In exercising justice, he intended the benefits of his people. Retribution in Deuteronomy is therefore not controlled or operated by any impersonal force but by God himself. It helps us to understand that disability is seen within the context of a divine relationship rather in the context of punishment. God, rather than the punishment itself, is the focus of the retribution. Secondly, God's faithfulness in keeping his people under his care and concern is another significant pillar of the retribution in Deuteronomy. He is not the one who is the source of sufferings but he stands with his people who face the complexities of life with lots of difficulties. The evidences of his faithfulness were seen time and again while bringing his people out of Egypt. Devine faithfulness assures his encouragement, comfort, and ever present-help towards people with disabilities. Thirdly, in Deuteronomy, God's compassion in Deuteronomy while bringing judgment shows his deep concern for his people. What men deserved as per their deeds was punishment. But God did not punish them. Instead of getting the punishment they were shown compassion. The purpose behind this was that people would repent and be restored. In the context of God's compassion and mercy, disabilities were not considered as punishment for the wrong doings of the past. Therefore, retribution in Deuteronomy offers the clear implication that disability is not because of sinful works of the past.

Thereafter, we had a comparative study between the law of *karma* and retribution in Deuteronomy. Firstly, we discovered that in the law of *karma* punishment for the sin is at the center whereas God Himself is at the center of retribution in Deuteronomy. Secondly, God is not involved in the the law of *karma* and the judgment is carried out by either an impersonal force or by an automatic principle. But the attitude of personal God is tied to retribution in Deuteronomy. Thirdly, the law of *karma* declares that the present situation is due to the sinful works of the previous birth and future birth will take place on the basis of the work of the present one. But in the retribution of Deuteronomy everything happens on this earth. God's compassion gives sinners the privilege to repent and live a life pleasing to God. It is significant to note that there are drastic differences between retribution in Deuteronomy and the law of *karma.*

Even though a link between the deeds of the past and the present consequences of men does not have strong connection in retribution in Deuteronomy, in the popular culture of India disabilities have been always been understood as caused by sin of the previous birth. This is because, the ideology of *karma* has had a tremendous influence upon the people of India, including Christians. To investigate whether Indian's general attitudes towards disabilities correlates with the principle of *karma* we looked at the popular culture of India in chapter 5.

To observe the general disposition of the Indian popular Hindu culture, we considered primarily popular media such as newspapers, magazine, Bollywood movies, YouTube and other related media. Daily newspapers reveal the strong relationship between disabilities and the widely prevailed stigma attached to them. Stigma and discrimination makes the life of the disabled going very tough. They are not only stigmatized but also oppressed and considered inauspicious. Women with disabilities are sexually abused and exploited. Children with disabilities are killed. It becomes more discouraging when even the government does not take steps to make a disabled-friendly environment and society. Bollywood movies not only entertain people but also demonstrate absolutely inhuman attitudes towards disabilities. They reveal that people with disabilities are cheated, deceived, ignored, condemned, and rejected in the Indian street and that even parents, school teachers have quite negative perspectives. Disabled people are considered unfortunate and useless in terms of their past, present and future. Such kinds of attitudes are developed because in people's mind there is a strong correlation between disabilities and the with the teaching of the law of *karma.*

However, surprisingly, Indian Christians also reveal the same attitudes towards disabilities as Hindus. To observe their attitudes, we looked at the preaching and teaching of several Indian Christians on You Tube. The preaching of these pastors relates sin and sickness. According to them sickness and diseases are the result of sin. Others associate diseases with a generational curse. Some other even believe that a person goes through disabilities due to bad *karma*. They are also too judgmental in their preaching. For them sin is not only the real reason behind diseases but it will also keep the person away from the kingdom of God and ruin the joy and comfort of life. Clearly the Indian Christians mindsets also subliminally influenced by the law of *karma* as it operates in Hinduism.

Hence, based on these observations and inferences in the above chapters, we infer that, with respect to the disabilities, the Old Testament does not explicitly relate sin with disabilities. Disabilities are neither considered as the result of sin nor seen as the punishment from God. Even in Christianity down through the centuries we did not find sin behind disabilities to be a dominant factor. However, the ideology of Indian Hindus has strongly linked sin with disabilities. They strongly believe that a particular person goes through disabilities due to the sin of the previous birth. Accordingly, they have developed quite negative towards disabilities. Unfortunately, Indian Christians have also demonstrated the same perceptions and attitudes towards disabilities. Therefore, at least Indian Christians need to let the

Old Testament teach them more helpful and Biblical attitudes towards people affected by disabilities. We believe that they will be greatly helped if they carefully study the Old Testament to develop Biblical attitudes towards people with disabilities.

APPENDIX 1

COMMENTARY ON BHAGAVAD GITA 4:7-8 BY VIVEKANANDA

The commentary on the Bhagavad Gita by Swami Vivekananda notes:

> In India, they have the same idea of the Incarnations of God. One of their great Incarnations, *Krishna*, whose grand sermon, the *Bhagavad-Gitâ*, some of you might have read, says, "Though I am unborn, of changeless nature, and Lord of beings, yet subjugating My *Prakriti*, I come into being by My own *Mâyâ*. Whenever virtue subsides and immorality prevails, then I body Myself forth. For the protection of the good, for the destruction of the wicked, and for the establishment of Dharma, I come into being, in every age." Whenever the world goes down, the Lord comes to help it forward; and so He does from time to time and place to place.[311]

311 Swami Vivekananda, *The complete work of Swami Vivekananda*, Vol. 4, Lectures and Discourses, Christ the Messenger, Accessed on August 20, 2017.

Life is short, but the soul is immortal and eternal, and one thing being certain, death, let us therefore take up a great ideal and give up our whole life to it. Let this be our determination, and may He, the Lord, who "comes again and again for the salvation of His own people", to quote from our scriptures — may the great *Krishna* bless us and lead us all to the fulfilment of our aims.[312]

Our prophet says that whenever evil and immortality prevail on earth, He will come down and support His children; and this He is doing from time to time and from place to place. And whenever on earth you see an extraordinary holy man trying to uplift humanity, know that He is in him.[313]

Whenever virtue subsides and vice prevails, I come down to help mankind," declares *Krishna*, in the *Bhagavad-Gitâ*. Whenever this world of ours, on account of growth, on account of added circumstances, requires a new adjustment, a wave of power comes; and as a man is acting on two planes, the spiritual and the material, waves of adjustment come on both planes.[314]

---

https://en.wikisource.org/wiki/The_Complete_Works_of_Swami_Vivekananda/Volume_4/Lectures_and_Discourses/Christ,_the_Messenger.

312 Swami Vivekananda, *The complete work of Swami Vivekananda*, Volume 3, Lectures from Colombo to Almora, The future of India, Accessed on August 20, 2017. https://en.wikisource.org/wiki/The_Complete_Works_of_Swami_Vivekananda/Volume_3/Lectures_from_Colombo_to_Almora/The_Future_of_India.

313 Swami Vivekananda, *The complete work of Swami Vivekananda*, Volume 8, Notes of Class talks and Lectures, Hindu and Christians, Accessed on August 20, 2017 https://en.wikisource.org/wiki/The_Complete_Works_of_Swami_Vivekananda/Volume_8/Notes_Of_Class_Talks_And_Lectures/Hindus_And_Christians.

314 Swami Vivekananda, *The complete work of Swami Vivekananda*, Volume 4, Lectures and Discourses, My Mastor, accessed on August 20, 2017. https://en.wikisource.org/wiki/The_Complete_Works_of_Swami_Vivekananda/Volume_4/Lectures_and_Discourses/My_Master.

Whenever virtue subsides, and wickedness raises its head, I manifest Myself to restore the glory of religion — are the words, O noble Prince, of the Eternal One in the holy *Gitâ*, striking the keynote of the pulsating ebb and flow of the spiritual energy in the universe.[315]

315 Swami Vivekananda, *The complete work of Swami Vivekananda*, Volume 4, Writings: Prose/Reply to the Address of the Maharaja khetri, Accessed on August 20, 2017. https://en.wikisource.org/wiki/The_Complete_Works_of_Swami_Vivekananda/Volume_4/Writings:_Prose/Reply_to_the_Address_of_the_Maharaja_of_Khetri.

BIBLIOGRAPHY

Books

Beates, Michael S. *Disability and The Gospel: How God Uses Our Brokenness to Display His Grace.* Wheaton: Crossway, 2012.

Boyd, Robin. *An Introduction to Indian Christian Theology.* Delhi: ISPCK, 2000, 244.

Crowder, Bill. "*Poor Choices and Mixed Opportunities: The Mistakes of king Saul.*" Grand Rapids: RBC Ministries, 2010.

Frankfort, Henry. *Kingship and the Gods: A Study of Ancient Near Eastern Religion as the integration of Society and Nature.* Chicago: The University of Chicago Press, 1978.

Gidoomal, Ram and Mike Fearon. *Karma 'n' Chips: The New Age of Asian Spirituality.* London: Wimbledon Publishing Company, 1988.

Gopalan, S. *Hindu Social Philosophy.* New Delhi: Wiley Estern Limited, 1979.

Gunn, David M. *The Fate of King Saul.* England: JOST Press, 1989.

Hiriyanna, M. *The Essentials of Indian Philosophy*. London: George Allen & Unwin, 1949.

Joshi, O. P. *Introduction to Hinduism*. New Delhi: Preach Publications, 1999.

Krishan, Yuvraj. *The Doctrine of Karma*. Delhi: Motilal Banarashidass Publishers Private Limited, 1997.

Lemaitre, Solange. *Hinduism*. trans. John Fransis Brown, New York: Hawthorne Books Publishers, 1959.

Martin, James D. *The Book of Judges*. Cambridge Bible Commentary, New York: Cambridge University Press, 1975.

Masih, Jagdhari. *The Role of Swami Chinmayananda in Revitalization of Hinduism and Reinterpretation of Christianity*. Culcutta: Punthi Pustak, 2000.

McCann, J. Clinton. *Judges: Interpretation: A Bible Commentary for Teaching and Preaching*. Louisville, KY: Westminster John Knox Press, 2011.

Nouwen, Henri J. M. *Adam: God's beloved*. New York: Orbis Books, 1997.

Olyan, Saul M. *Disability in the Hebrew Bible: Interpreting Mental and Physical Differences*. New York: Cambridge University Press, 2008.

Schipper, Jeremy. *Disability Studies and The Hebrew Bible*. New York: T&T Clark, 2006.

Sharma, Arvind. *Classical Hindu Thought: An Introduction,* New Delhi: Oxford University Press, 2000.

Speiser, E. A. *Genesis*, AB. New York: Doubleday & Company Inc,1985.

Viswanathan, Ed. *Am I a Hindu?* New Delhi: Rupa & Co, 1993.

Yong, Amos. *The Bible, Disability and The Church*. Grand Rapids: William B. Eerdmans Publishing Company, 2011.

Younger, Paul and Susanna Oommen Younger. *Hinduism*. Niles Illinois: Argus communications, 1978.

Articles from Books

Baden, Joel S. "The Nature of Bareness in the Hebrew Bible," In Disability Studies and Biblical Literature, edited by Candida R. Moss and Jeremy Schipper, 13-28. United States: A division of St. Martin's press LLC, 2011.

Caspary, Almut. "The Patristic Era: Early Christian Attitudes Toward the Disfigured Outcast," *in Disability in the Christian Tradition: A Reader*, edited by Brain Brock and John Swinton, 24-64. Grand Rapids: William B. Eerdmans Publishing Company, 2012.

Cowans, Gordon "Towards A Liberatory Theology of Disability: Humanity in Creation, Disability and the Image of God," *in Doing Theology from Disability Perspective: A Theological Resource Book on Disability*, edited by Wati Longchar and Gordon Cowans 149-156. Philippines: The Association for Theological Education in South East Asia, 2011.

Creamer, Deborah Beth. "John Calvin and Disability," *in Disability in the Christian Tradition: A Reader,* edited by Brain Brock and John Swinton 216-250. Grand Rapids: William B. Eerdmans Publishing Company, 2012.

Durai, A. Arumai. "The Church and the Otherwise-abled: A Historical Overview" *in Embracing the Inclusive Community: A Disability Perspective*, edited by A. Wati Longchar and R. Christopher Rajkumar, 17-33. Bangalore: BTESSC/SATHRI, NCCI & SCEPTRE, 2010.

Heuser, Stefan "The Human Condition as Seen from the Cross: Luther and Disability" *in Disability in the Christian Tradition: A Reader*, edited by Brain Brock and John Swinton 184-215. Grand Rapids: William B. Eerdmans Publishing Company, 2012.

Jeyakumar, Arthur. "The Early Church and Persons with Disability," *in Sprouts of Disability Theology*, edited by Christopher Rajkumar 44-47. Nagpur: National Council of Churches in India, 2012.

Kabue, Samuel N. "Church and Society's Response to Disability: Historical and Sociological Perspective" *in Doing Theology from Disability Perspective: A Theological Resource Book on Disability*, edited by Wati Longchar and Gordon Cowans, 119-131. Philippines: The Association for Theological Education in South East Asia, 2011.

Kabue, Samuel. "Ecumenical Disability Advocates Network (EDAN)" *in Doing Theology from Disability Perspective: A Theological Resource Book on Disability*, edited by Wati Longchar and Gordon Cowans, 72-78. Philippines: The Association for Theological Education in South East Asia, 2011.

Kelley, Nicole. "The punishment of the Body was Apparent in the Torment of the Human Body: Epilepsy in Ancient Christianity" *in Disability Studies and Biblical Literature*, edited by Candida R. Moss and Jeremy Schipper, 205-221. United States: Palgrave Macmillan, 2011.

Longchar, Wati. "Culture, Sin, Suffering and Disability in Society" *in Doing Theology from Disability Perspective: A Theological Resource Book on Disability*, edited by Wati Longchar and Gordon Cowans 175-187. Philippines: The Association for Theological Education in South East Asia, 2011.

Murry, Ezamo. "Experiencing the Disable Diety" *In Sprouts of Disability Theology,* edited by. Christopher Rajkumar, Chennai: National Council of Churches in India, 2012.

Murry, Ezamo. "Some Aspects in Psychology of the Person with Disability" *in Doing Theology from Disability Perspective: A Theological Resource Book on Disability*, edited by Wati Longchar and Gordon Cowans, 228-236. Philippines: The Association for Theological Education in South East Asia, 2011.

Reynolds Thomas E. "The Cult of Normalcy" In *Disability: Christian Reflection*, edited by. Robert B. Kruschwitz, 25-33, Waco: The Center for Christian Ethics Baylor University, 2012.

Skoda, Hannah. "Representation of Disability in the Thirteenth-Century Miracles de Saint Louis" *in Disability in the Middle ages: Reconsideration and Reverberation*, edited by Joshua R. Eyler, 53-66. Great Britain: MPG books Groups, 2010.

Swinton, John "Many Bodies, Many Worlds" In *Disability: Christian Reflection*, edited by Robert B. Kruschwitz 18-24, Waco: The Center for Christian Ethics Baylor University, 2012.

Thomson, Rod "Mephi Bosheth at the table: A High Point in Davidic Kingship-2 Samuel 9:1-13" *In Theology and the Experience of Disability*, edited by Andrew Picard and Myk Habets 145-151, New York: Routledge Taylor & Francis Group, 2016.

Wells, Scoot. "The Exemplary Blindness of Francis of Assisi", *in Disability in the Middle ages: Reconsideration and Reverberation*, edited by Joshua R. Eyler, 67-80. Great Britain: MPG books Groups, 2010.

Yong, Amos. "Disability and the Love of Wisdom: Deforming, Re-forming and Per-forming Philosophy of Religion" *in Disability in Judaism, Christianity and Islam*, edited by Darla Schumm and Michael Stoltzfus 205-227. New York: Palgrave Macmillan, 2011.

Articles from Journal

Amirav, Anna Goldman. "Behold the LORD has Restrained Me from Bearing" *Journal of International Feminist Analysis* 1, no. 3 (1988).

Andrus, David. "A Theological Evaluation of Disability", *Missio Apostolica* 18, no. 2 (2010): 121-131.

Andrus, David. "Theology and its Impact on People with Disability: An Ecclesiology Inclusive of People with a Disability" *Missio Apostolica* 18, no. 2 (Nov. 2010): 142-148.

Arion, Alexandru Corneliu. "The Essence of Hindu Doctrine and its Influence on Christianity in America and Europe."

International Journal of Orthodox Theolgy 6, no. 4 (2014): 163-210.

Avioz, Michael. "The Motif of Beauty in the Books of Samuel and kings" *Vetus Testamentum* 59 (2009): 341-349.

Ball, Robert. "Christian Leadership and the Crippling Effect of Narcissism: A Historical Intertexture Analysis of Judges 13-16" *Journal of Biblical Perspectives in Leadership* 6, no. 1 (2014): 16-26.

Beckenstein, Amanda "Samson's Body Politic" *Biblical Interpretation* 20 (2012): 389-406.

Blanks A Brooke and J. David Smith, "Multiculturalism, Religion and Disability: Implications for special Education Practitioners" *Educational and training in Developmental Disabilities* 44, no. 3 (2009): 295-303.

Bloomfield, Elana. "Conceiving Motherhood: The Jewish Female Body in Israeli Reproductive practices" *Intersections* 10, no. 2 (Spring 2009): 227-271.

Bruce, Patricia. "Constructions of Disability Ancient and Modern: The Impact of Religious Belief on the Experience of Disability" *Neotestamentica* 44, no. 2 (2010): 253-281.

Chakraborty, Poulami. "The law of *karma* and Salvation", *International Journal of Humanities and Social Science Studies* 1, no. III (2014): 192-195.

Chapman, Stephen B., Reading the Bible as Witness: Divine Retribution in the Old Testament." *Perspectives in Religious Studies* 31, no. 2 (2004): 171-190.

Clapton, Jayne. "Disability, Inclusion and the Christian Church: Practice, Paradox and Promise", *Disability and Rehabilitation* 19, no.10 (1997): 420-426.

Creamer, Deborah Beth. "Re-reading Calvin and disability", *Journal of Religion, Disability and Health 17*, no. 3 (2013): 281-286.

Cundall, Arther E. "Sacral King-The Old Testament Background" *Vox Evangelica* 6 (1969): 31-41.

Cusack Carole M. "Graciosi: Medieval Christian Attitudes to Disability" *Disability and Rehabilitation* 19, no. 10 (1997): 414-419.

Dekker, John. "May the Lord Make the Woman like Rachel" *Tyndale Bulletin* 64, no. 1 (2013): 17-32.

Deuel, David "God's Story of Disability: The Unfolding Plan from Genesis to Revelation," *JCID* 2, no. 2 (Fall/Winter 2013): 81-96.

Dyrness, William A. "Aesthetics in the Old Testament: Beauty in Context" *JETS* 28, no. 4 (December 1985): 421-432.

Eiesland, Nancy. "Encountering the Disabled God" *PMLA* 120, no. 2 (Mar., 2005): 584-586.

Gammie, John G. "Theology of Retribution in the Book of Deuteronomy." *The Catholic Biblical Quarterly* 32.1 (1970): 1-12.

Ganapathi, Bonela "Rehabilitation for the Disabled Person" *International Journal of Multidiciplinary Research Trends* III, no. 3 (July 2016): 51-62.

Ganesh, Gayatri. Chris Merin Varghese. "Mobility Devices for the Physically Disabled: A Story of Hope from Chhattisgarh, Central India", *Dharma Deepika* 20, no. 1 (January-June 2016): 20-30.

Geoffrey David Miller, "Attitudes Towards Dogs in Ancient Israel: A Reassessment" *Journal of the Study of the Old Testament 32*, no. 4 (2008): 487-500.

Ghai, Anita. "Disabled Women: An Excluded Agenda of Indian Feminism" *Hypatia* 17, no.3, (Summer 2002): 49-66.

Green, Mark. "Enigma Variations: Aspects of Samson Story Judges 13-16." *Vox Evangelica* 21 (1992): 53-80.

Havrelock, Rachel. "The Myth of Birthing the Hero: Heroic Barrenness in the Hebrew Bible" *Biblical Interpretation* 16, (2008): 154-178.

Hawk, L. Daniel. "Cast Out and Cast off: Hagar, Leah and the God who sees" *Priscilla Papers* 25, no. 1 (Winter 2011): 9-13.

Howard, David M. "The Case for Kingship in the Old Testament Narrative books and the Psalms" *Trinity Journal 9,* (1988): 19-35.

Hubbard, Robert L. "The Eyes Have It: Theological Reflections on human beauty" *Ex auditu* 13 (1997): 57-72.

Johnson, Benjamin J. M. "What Type of Son is Samson? Reading Judges 13 as a Biblical Type-Scene" *JETS* 53, no. 2 (June 2010): 269-286.

Joze krasovec, Joze. "Is There a Doctrine of Collective Retribution in the Hebrew Bible" *Hebrew Union College Annual* 65 (1995): 35-89.

Junior Nyasha and Jeremy Schipper, "Mosaic Disability and Identity in Exodus 4:10; 6:12, 30" *Biblical Interpretation* 16 (2008): 428-441.

Koblitz, Daniel C. "Theology and Disability: Reexamining Scripture as it Applies to Stuttering" *Journal of the Christian Institute of Disability* 51, no. 1 (Spring/summer 2016): 31-52.

Krasovec. Joze. "Is There a Doctrine of Collective Retribution in the Hebrew Bible" *Hebrew Union College Annual* 65 (1995): 35-89.

Ledgerwood, Elaine. "Saint not Sinners: An Investigation into the "Positive" Constructions of Disability by the Historical Church", *Colloquim* 42, no. 1 (May 2010): 85-98.

McConville, J Gordon. "Retribution in Deuteronomy: Theology and Ethics" *Interpretation: A journal of Bible and Theology* 63. no. 3 (2015): 288-292.

Miles, M. "Disability in an Eastern Religious Context: Historical Perspectives" *Disability and Society* 10, no. 1 (1995): 49-69.

Prakash A. Praveen, J. Esther Jerlin and P. Anitha "Dominant Problems of Rural Deprived Persons with Disability Using Fuzzy Cluster Analysis." Proceeding of the World Congress on Engineering 1 (July 2-4, 2014): np.

Rouse, Christopher D. "Scripture and the Disabled: Redeeming Mephibosheth's Identity" *Journal of Pentecostal Theology* 17 (2008): 183-199.

Singh, J. P. "Changing Attitudes A Paradigm Shift in Perception: Focus on disability Studies" *Delhi Psychiatry Journal 13*, no.1, (April 2010): 101-108.

Slight, Camille W. "A Hero of Conscience: Samson Agonistes and Casuistry" *Modern Language Association* 90, no. 3 (May 1975): 395-413.

Smith, Michael J. "The Failure of the Family in Judges, Part 2: Samson" *Bibliotheca Sacra* 162 (October-December 2006): 424-436.

Ventura, Charles Savona, "Reproductive Issue in the Torah" *Malta Medical Journal* 27, no. 2 (2015): 47-53.

Wall, Benjamin S. "Disability in Christian Tradition: A Reader Theological Contributions to Disability Course" *Ethics in Brief* 19, no. 2 (2013): np.

White, Kayla. "The Legal Status of barren Women in the Ancient Near East" *Priscilla Papers* 28, no. 4 (2014): 18-22.

Whitman, Sarah M. "Pain and Suffering as Viewed by the Hindu Religion", *The Journal of Pain* 8, no. 8 (August 2007): 607-613.

Zimran, Yisca. "The Lord Has Rejected you as King over Israel: Saul's Deposal from the Throne" *Journal of Hebrew Scripture* 14, no. 5 (2014): 1-9.

Newspaper Articles

"26-yr-old woman poisons disabled son kills herself", The times of India City, August 13, 2017, Accessed on 10.9.2017 http://timesofindia.indiatimes.com/city/coimbatore/26-yr-old-woman-poisons-disabled-son-kills-herself/articleshow/60039711.cms.

"Disabled and Disheartened", The Hindu, July 06, 2016, Accessed on 12.9.2017, http://www.thehindu.com/opinion/editorial/Disabled-and-disheartened/article14472708.ece.

"Disabled boy's testimony sent sex offender to jail", The Times of India City, August 05, 2017, Accessed on 14.09.2017, http://timesofindia.indiatimes.com/city/delhi/disabled-boys-testimony-sends-sex-offender-to-jail/articleshow/59923083.cms.

Anand, Ayushi. "First Physically Challenged Women to Top IAS, Ira Singhal tells how her Disability was never an Excuse" *India Today,* May 9, 2016. http://indiatoday.intoday.in/education/story/ias-topper-interview/1/663575.html.

Balachandran, Manu. "India treats its mentally disabled worse than animals", Quartz India, December 3. 2014, https://qz.com/306299/india-treats-its-mentally-disabled-worse-than-animals/.

Banerjee, Poulomi. "Disabled women not thought to be wife material by many", Hindustan Times, January 08, 2017, http://www.hindustantimes.com/india-news/disabled-women-not-thought-to-be-wife-material-by-many/story-QMqdQ4CSo43GQg5diavRGL.html.

Ghunawat, Virendrasingh. "PMO ignored 'opened letter' and complained made by disabled girl, instead passed the buck to MEA", *India Today*, January 22, 2017. http://indiatoday.intoday.in/story/pmo-ignored-open-letter-and-complain-made-by-disabled-girl-instead-passed-the-buck-to-mea/1/863411.html.

Harris,Trudy. "Stigma thrives for India's 60 million disabled" The Hindu, February 21, 2014, Accessed on 13.09.2017, https://www.dawn.com/news/1088491.

Hemani Bhandari, Hemani. "Mentally Challenged Women Raped", The Hindu, July 4. 2017. http://www.thehindu.com/news/cities/Delhi/mentally-challenged-woman-raped/article19206569.ece.

Jha, Martand. "Disabilities and the Culture of Violence", The Hindu, February 7, 2017. Accessed on 13.09.2017, http://www.thehindu.com/todays-paper/tp-opinion/Disability-and-the-culture-of-violence/article17206805.ece.

Killalea, Debra. "India's Shame: The Women 'Treated Worse than Animal" news.com au. Dec. 4.2014, http://www.news.com.au/lifestyle/real-life/true-stories/indias-shame-the-women-treated-worse-than-animals/news-story/cb5e838172ee7aeb86a83354afb296d3.

Mascarenhas, Anuradha "Women with disabilities Locked away, abused: HRW Report", Indian Express, December 05.2014. http://indianexpress.com/article/cities/pune/women-with-disabilities-locked-away-abused-hrw-report/.

Sarkar, Monica. "Disability in India: The struggles of infrastructure, prejudice and karma", CNN, December 27, 2013.http://edition.cnn.com/2013/12/27/world/asia/india-disability-challenges/index.html.

Satyamev Jayate, "Satyamev Jayate S1I Episode 6 I Person with Disabilities I full Episode (Hindi)" You Tube Video, 1:04:30, June 9, 2012. https://www.youtube.com/watch?v=39SNcM99o4Q.

Shreedharan, Divya. "My Body has Also Needs", The Hindu, May 9, 2015. http://www.thehindu.com/features/magazine/my-body-also-has-needs/article7184098.ece.

Thomas, Rosamma. "Sahariya Worried for Disabled Daughter, no help from Government", The times of India City, July 27, 2017, http://timesofindia.indiatimes.com/city/jaipur/sahariya-worried-for-disabled-daughter-no-help-from-government/articleshow/59794570.cms.

Movies

Bhatt, Ban. *Dosti*, Directed by Satyen Bose, performed by Sudhir Kumar Sawant, Sushil Kumar Somaya (1964, India: Tarachand Barjatya, Rajshri production,1964), Film.

Gupte, Amole. *Tare Zameen Par,* Directed by Amir Khan, performed by Darsheel Safary, Amir Khan, (2007, India: Amir Khan Production, 2007), Film.

Quora

Agrawall, Shraddha. "The attitude towards disabled in India is very dismal. What do you think the problem is?" Quora, June 18, 2016, https://www.quora.com/The-attitude-towards-disabled-in-India-is-very-dismal-What-do-you-think-the-problem-is.

Modi, Virali. "The attitude towards disabled in India is very dismal. What do you think the problem is?" Quora, June 13, 2016. 06.09.2017, https://www.quora.com/The-attitude-towards-disabled-in-India-is-very-dismal-What-do-you-think-the-problem-is.

YouTube Videos

Adonai International Ministries Bangalore, "Pastor Santosh Prabhu-Jesus can turn Curses into Blessing, English & Kannada" YouTube video, 28:19, March 16, 2015, https://www.youtube.com/watch?v=orYGE3csAbE.

Christian sermons, "Sin-Part-1-Malayalam Christian Message by Pr K. Joy," You tube video, 1:03.18 April 24, 2013, https://www.youtube.com/watch?v=rvAe-5Sn84k.

God is One Only Jesus, "The Effect of sin (part 1) A sermon by Apostle Ankur Narula", YouTube video, 22:34 June 23, 2017, https://www.youtube.com/watch?v=-vKQFYksp2g.

jeddyboy03, "Sin of Foolishness P 2", YouTube video, 7:41, November 19, 2009, https://www.youtube.com/watch?v=ezObHOOPUGc.

Jesus Calls, "Forgiving sin (English-Hindi) -Bro. DGS. Dhinakaran", YouTube video, 9:44, November 12, 2016, https://www.youtube.com/watch?v=Gy0-ZyAdmUI.

lovejesusdivine "Preaching by Fr. Joseph Edattu (English)" YouTube video, 9:15, April 18, 2013, https://www.youtube.com/watch?v=imFq2w4zfLo.

Masihi Geet HD "Sin Destroys your Comfort But Forgiveness is from Jesus Only, Apostle Ankur Narula," YouTube video, 20:19, May 20, 2007, https://www.youtube.com/watch?v=DUb0xsKL7F8.

MIRACLEHEALING CENTRE, "How to Dominate Sickness and Disease", YouTube video, 50:17, March 16, 2012, https://www.youtube.com/watch?v=hxU9ziYjX44.

Pillai Center, "Ultimate teachings: Sick body is dangerous" YouTube video, 4:10, teaching, August 11, 2015. https://www.youtube.com/watch?v=6G0P5QkLp3Y.

Point of View "Disability in India I Everyday Problems I Point of View, YouTube video, 6:40, February 3, 2017, https://www.youtube.com/watch?v=qdxqDNWqb_E.

Prayer Mansion, "Warning to People Who Criticizes God's Servant-Bro. DGS. Dhinakaran" YouTube video, 5:25 July 1, 2013, https://www.youtube.com/watch?v=YqxaXX228xU.

SermonIndex.net "Why God Allows His Children to Suffer by Zac Poonem", YouTube Video, 58:08, March 19, 2011, https://www.youtube.com/watch?v=17Dc18Zkc_Q.

Shubhsandeshtv, "Shyam Kishor I God's Will is to Heal Every one! I Part 1I09," YouTube Video, 28:34, September 11, 2015, https://www.youtube.com/watch?v=2SQHLUV41Es.

Tube Buddies, "Documentary on Disability in India" You Tube video, 6:47, November 15, 2016, https://www.youtube.com/watch?v=nl3-K_3MkJQ.

Word of life Church, "Jesus vs. Karma I Pastor Brain Zahnd I Word of life church" YouTube video, 36:03, July 9, 2013, https://www.youtube.com/watch?v=vK3UOpir6SY.

Online Sources

"Bhagavad Gita Chapter 4, Verse 7-8: Yada Yada Hi Dharmasya" *Swami Vivekananda Quotes*, Accessed on August 20, 2017, http://www.swamivivekanandaquotes.org/2014/05/bhagavad-gita-chapter-4-verse-7-8.html.

Swami Vivekananda, *The complete work of Swami Vivekananda*, Volume 4, Lectures and Discourses, Christ the Messenger, accessed on August 20, 2017. https://en.wikisource.org/wiki/The_Complete_Works_of_Swami_Vivekananda/Volume_4/Lectures_and_Discourses/Christ,_the_Messenger.

Swami Vivekananda, *The complete work of Swami Vivekananda*, Volume 3, Lectures from Colombo to Almora, The future of India, Accessed on August 20,2017. https://en.wikisource.org/wiki/The_Complete_Works_of_Swami_Vivekananda/Volume_3/Lectures_from_Colombo_to_Almora/The_Future_of_India.

Swami Vivekananda, *The complete work of Swami Vivekananda*, Volume 8, Notes of Class talks and Lectures, Hindu and Christians, Accessed on August 20, 2017. https://en.wikisource.org/wiki/The_Complete_Works_of_Swami_Vivekananda/Volume_8/Notes_Of_Class_Talks_And_Lectures/Hindus_And_Christians.

Swami Vivekananda, *The complete work of Swami Vivekananda*, Volume 4, Lectures and Discourses, My Mastor, accessed on August 20, 2017. https://en.wikisource.org/wiki/The_Complete_Works_of_Swami_Vivekananda/Volume_4/Lectures_and_Discourses/My_Master.

Swami Vivekananda, *The complete work of Swami Vivekananda*, Volume 4, Writings: Prose/Reply to the Address of the Maharaja khetri, Accessed on August 20, 2017. https://en.wikisource.

org/wiki/The_Complete_Works_of_Swami_Vivekananda/Volume_4/Writings:_Prose/Reply_to_the_Address_of_the_Maharaja_of_Khetre.

Unpublished Sources

Dharamraj, Havilah. "Boldly Go: Tracking Trends in Comparative Literature" to be published in a forthcoming book, 3.

Kartik Pal is a graduate of SAIACS, Bangalore (M.Th.) and Presbyterian Theological Seminary Dehradun (M.Div.). has been in teaching ministry since 2004.